CISTERCIAN STUDIES SERIES: NUMBER TWO HUNDRED SIXTY-SIX

Thomas Merton
Early Essays, 1947–1952

CISTERCIAN STUDIES SERIES: NUMBER TWO HUNDRED SIXTY-SIX

Thomas Merton

Early Essays, 1947–1952

Edited with an Introduction by
Patrick F. O'Connell

Foreword by
Jonathan Montaldo

α

Cistercian Publications
www.cistercianpublications.org

LITURGICAL PRESS
Collegeville, Minnesota
www.litpress.org

A Cistercian Publications title published by Liturgical Press

Cistercian Publications
Editorial Offices
161 Grosvenor Street
Athens, Ohio 54701
www.cistercianpublications.org

1   2   3   4   5   6   7   8   9

Library of Congress Cataloging-in-Publication Data

Merton, Thomas, 1915–1968.
    [Essays. Selections]
    Thomas Merton : early essays, 1947–1952 / by Thomas Merton ; edited by Patrick F. O'Connell ; foreword by Jonathan Montaldo.
        pages   cm. — (Cistercian studies ; number two hundred sixty-six)
    Includes bibliographical references.
    Summary: "This volume gathers together twelve essays that Thomas Merton wrote for various journals between 1947 and 1952, the years that saw the publication of his best-selling autobiography The Seven Storey Mountain, his ordination to the priesthood, and his initial appointment as spiritual and intellectual guide of the young monks at the Abbey of Gethsemani. The essays, most of which have never been reprinted, focus above all on aspects of the contemplative life but also consider the spiritual dimensions of literature and the social implications of Christian life. Issued to coincide with the one hundredth anniversary of his birth, this collection brings to fruition at long last Merton's own original plan of publishing these essays as a group and so makes available a previously little recognized and underutilized resource for understanding and appreciating a crucial transitional phase in his life as both monk and writer." — Provided by publisher.
        ISBN 978-0-87907-266-7 (paperback) — ISBN 978-0-87907-496-8 (ebook)
        1. Contemplation.   2. Spiritual life—Catholic Church.   I. O'Connell, Patrick F., editor.   II. Title.

BV5091.C7M46   2015
248.4'82—dc23
                                                                2014048630

Contents

vi *Contents*

Foreword

The publication in 2013 of Thomas Merton's *Selected Essays*,[1] each essay being carefully explicated in the context of Merton's biographical and literary development by Patrick F. O'Connell, was a major event in recent presentations of Merton's work. That volume of 512 pages provides ample evidence of Merton's skillful and capacious intelligence in his assaying a variety of topics that arrested him throughout his writer's life. Now complementing his selection of the finest examples of Merton's work as essayist, O'Connell has turned his attention to Merton's early forays into writing for Catholic magazines in the latter part of the 1940s.

The monk who writes these early essays is not yet the Catholic household name he would become after the publication of his autobiography *The Seven Storey Mountain* in 1948.[2] While they do not compete with his mature work, these initial essays, collected together for the first time, valuably expose Merton's appropriation of the classical and traditional sources that point to the significance of contemplation as the goal of all Christian living. In these dozen essays, Merton imbues his words with the perceived force of authority gained not only through intense study but also through personal experience as he enumerates the decisions to be enacted by all Christians so as to eschew the claims of materialism, the

---

[1] Thomas Merton, *Selected Essays*, ed. Patrick F. O'Connell (Maryknoll, NY: Orbis Books, 2013).

[2] Thomas Merton, *The Seven Storey Mountain* (New York: Harcourt, Brace, 1948).

"spirit of the world," and convert their minds and hearts toward union with God. In a remarkable essay, "Contemplation in a Rocking Chair," Merton unsparingly outlines the necessary acts of continuing renunciation required by any Christian who hopes to receive the gift of gifts, the grace of "infused contemplation," through which God is perceived as directly as is possible to a human being on this side of eternity. His attack on a style of Christian meditation and living that might be called "contemplation lite" becomes a consistent Merton emphasis in all his later teaching. He always emphasizes that no technique of meditation can evade the rigorous discipline of enduring dark nights of the soul. Merton never declares that the true contemplative is happy and a satisfied success, or that the journey to contemplation allows anyone to be all right with the world.

After only six years of monastic living at Gethsemani, Merton began to teach in these essays and publicly to hand on to others his own existential grasp of what must be sacrificed and abandoned if one is to be graced with "infused contemplation," which he defined as "an experimental knowledge of God's goodness 'tasted' and 'possessed' by a vital contact in the depths of the soul. By infused love, we are given an immediate grasp of God's own substance, and rest in the obscure and profound sense of His presence and transcendent actions within our inmost selves, yielding ourselves altogether to the work of His transforming Spirit" (6). Merton never abandoned this ideal but to his mind literally understood formulation. He deepened and expanded his definition of infused contemplation in his books *The Climate of Monastic Prayer*[3] and *The Inner Experience*[4] and in the essays published as *Contemplation in a World of Action*,[5] but he never abandoned his belief that

[3] Thomas Merton, *The Climate of Monastic Prayer* (Washington, DC: Cistercian Publications, 1969); also published as Thomas Merton, *Contemplative Prayer* (New York: Herder & Herder, 1969).

[4] Thomas Merton, *The Inner Experience: Notes on Contemplation*, ed. William H. Shannon (San Francisco: HarperCollins, 2003).

[5] Thomas Merton, *Contemplation in a World of Action* (Garden City, NY: Doubleday, 1971).

contemplation as surrendering to the work of the transforming Spirit is the goal of every person's spiritual practice. His personal journals, his poetry, and his correspondence with others provide ample clues to his own inner experiences of "God's goodness" and his own "vital contact" with God's mercy in "the depths" of his soul. The voice in these first public essays is young, but to anyone who has long pondered Merton's mature writing on contemplation it is immediately recognizable.

Merton's personal journals for the years 1945–1952, presented under the title *Entering the Silence,*[6] provide clues to the climate of inner turmoil Merton experienced in these years, which helps to explain his consistent, publicly stated sense of a conflict of interest between his desires to be a literary artist and a contemplative monk. Even before he entered Gethsemani in 1941, he intuited (if only tentatively, because he did not destroy all his premonastic writing but entrusted it to others) that he would have to renounce vocalizing his "false self"—the artist who wanted fame by communicating the sound of his own voice—in order to discover his "truer self" in contemplation, as a monk who listened in silence for a voice that was not his own. Even as he longed to be silent so that the voice of Christ could utter itself in him, he found himself inexorably caught up in the adulation of his readers and all the business that attends a prominent literary career.

One of the most important essays in this volume is "Poetry and the Contemplative Life," in which Merton presents the goals of the artist-poet and those of the contemplative as incompatible. In this article's formal pronouncements, Merton lays bare the knot within his inner experience that in time might have been loosened but never fully untied:

> Now it is precisely here that the esthetic instinct changes its colors and, from being a precious gift becomes a *fatal handicap.* If the intuition of the poet naturally leads him into the inner sanctuary of his soul, it is for a special purpose in the natural

[6] Thomas Merton, *Entering the Silence: Becoming a Monk and Writer. Journals,* vol. 2: *1941–1952,* ed. Jonathan Montaldo (San Francisco: HarperCollins, 1996).

order: when the poet enters into himself, it is in order to reflect
upon his inspiration and to clothe it with a special and splendid form and then return to *display it to those outside*. And here
the radical difference between the artist and the mystic begins
to be seen. The artist enters into himself in order to *work*. For
him, the "superior" soul is a forge where inspiration kindles
a fire of white heat, a crucible for the transformation of natural
images into new, created forms. But the mystic enters into
himself, not in order to work but to pass through the center
of his own soul and lose himself in the mystery and secrecy
and infinite, transcendent reality of God living and working
within him.

Consequently, if the mystic happens to be, at the same time,
an artist, when prayer calls him within himself to the secrecy
of God's presence, his art will be tempted to start working
and producing and studying the "creative" possibilities of
this experience. And therefore immediately the whole thing
runs the risk of being frustrated and destroyed. The artist will
be cheated of a gift of tremendous and supernatural worth,
and be left with nothing—but the experience of an artist. And
instead of passing through the sanctuary of his own soul into
the abyss of the infinite actuality of God Himself, he will
remain there a moment, only to emerge again into the exterior
world of multiple created things whose variety once more
dissipates his energies until they are lost in perplexity and
dissatisfaction. (14)

Here is the literary clue to Merton's inner experiences of his own
bad faith, his "dread," as he explains it in *The Climate of Monastic
Prayer*. He is consistently disappointed with himself for only being
a writer who can write beautifully about the contemplative life
without achieving the contemplation that is the goal of Christian
life. To his credit, Merton deeply realized, even on his first tasting
of artistic achievement in the profession of his autobiography, that
the greatest threat to receiving the grace of contemplation is
celebrity. He intuited from the start that his desire to teach on
contemplation would be undercut by any of his unstated desires
to become a Christian guru. Repeatedly in the journals collected
in *Entering the Silence*, Merton warns himself that his new-won
fame and the nascent formation of a cult of personality around his

literary self by his readers would be the flaming sword that barred him from passing "through the center of his own soul [so as to] lose himself in the mystery and secrecy and infinite, transcendent reality of God living and working within him" (14).

In his essay "The Contemplative Life: Its Meaning and Necessity," Merton enunciates his enduring faith, for which he was criticized by some, that "Contemplation is the fullness of the Christian life. It is the deep and supernatural and perfect experience of God, which we were all created to enjoy in heaven and which those who listen to God, on earth, and make the sacrifices which He asks of them, may taste even before they enter into heaven: *quaedam inchoatio vitae eternae* (a certain beginning of eternal life—St. Thomas)" .(108). He always counters this faith, however, by recognizing that the gift of the "perfect experience of God" (108) is only granted to those who by ascetic renunciations have separated themselves "from the violence and greed and injustice and cruelty of this world, with all its noise and shallow appeals to passion and its crass stupidity" (115). Contemplation for Merton never becomes a passive and "soft way." It is hard and only for those who long for the gift of God's presence within them by "penance, renouncement and prayer" (115).

Obviously these essays have started my engines. I would say more, but my enthusiasm for these topics in Merton's writing has already led me to exceed the bounds of a brief foreword to an important work. Yet I cannot close without acknowledging the debt any serious reader of Thomas Merton owes to the scholarship of Patrick F. O'Connell. His annotations to Merton's teaching conferences in particular, numbering seven volumes in the Monastic Wisdom Series of Cistercian Publications,[7] are a *tour de force* of

[7] Thomas Merton, *Cassian and the Fathers: Initiation into the Monastic Tradition*, ed. Patrick F. O'Connell, MW 1 (Kalamazoo, MI: Cistercian Publications, 2005); Thomas Merton, *Pre-Benedictine Monasticism: Initiation into the Monastic Tradition 2*, ed. Patrick F. O'Connell, MW 9 (Kalamazoo, MI: Cistercian Publications, 2006); Thomas Merton, *An Introduction to Christian Mysticism: Initiation into the Monastic Tradition 3*, ed. Patrick F. O'Connell, MW 13 (Kalamazoo, MI: Cistercian Publications, 2008); Thomas Merton, *The Rule of Saint Benedict: Initiation into the Monastic Tradition 4*, ed. Patrick F. O'Connell, MW 19 (Collegeville, MN: Cistercian Publications, 2009); Thomas Merton, *Monastic Observances: Initiation*

detail, wide learning, and impeccable scholarship that brings Merton's conference notes alive, rendering them cogent and important for a contemporary audience. In Patrick F. O'Connell, Merton's writing has found one of its most gifted readers and interpreters. I praise his achievements without fear of challenge and wish him many more years of continued good work.

Jonathan Montaldo

---

into the Monastic Tradition 5, ed. Patrick F. O'Connell, MW 25 (Collegeville, MN: Cistercian Publications, 2010); Thomas Merton, *The Life of the Vows: Initiation into the Monastic Tradition 6*, ed. Patrick F. O'Connell, MW 30 (Collegeville, MN: Cistercian Publications, 2012); Thomas Merton, *Charter, Customs, and Constitutions of the Cistercians: Initiation into the Monastic Tradition 7*, ed. Patrick F. O'Connell, MW 41 (Collegeville, MN: Cistercian Publications, 2015).

Acknowledgments

"States of Life" by Fr. John Fearon, OP, *The Thomist* 12, no. 1 (January 1949): 1–16. Used by permission of *The Thomist*.

Journal entries for January 22, 24, 26, 1949 (pp. 266–70: 1,912 words) from ENTERING THE SILENCE: THE JOURNALS OF THOMAS MERTON VOLUME TWO 1941–1952 by THOMAS MERTON and EDITED BY JONATHAN MONTALDO. Copyright © 1995 by The Merton Legacy Trust. Reprinted by permission of Harper Collins Publishers.

The following articles have been reprinted by permission of the Merton Legacy Trust:

"The Trappists Go to Utah," *Commonweal* (August 29, 1947)

"Death of a Trappist," *Integrity* (November 1947)

"A Christmas Devotion," *Commonweal* (December 26, 1947)

"A Trappist Speaks on People, Priests and Prayer," *The Messenger of the Sacred Heart* (April 1948)

"Contemplation in a Rocking Chair," *Integrity* (August 1948)

"Is Mysticism Normal," *Commonweal* (November 4, 1949)

"The Contemplative Life: Its Meaning and Necessity," *The Dublin Review* (Winter 1949)

"The Primacy of Contemplation," *Cross and Crown* (March 1950)

"Christ Suffers Again," *Action Now!* (March 1952)

"Poetry and the Contemplative Life"

"Active and Contemplative Orders"

The following permissions were in process at the time of publication:

From Farrar, Straus, and Giroux: Thomas Merton, "Self-Denial and the Christian."

From Harcourt, Brace: Thomas Merton, "Active and Contemplative Orders."

Introduction

On November 5, 1947, Thomas Merton wrote to his friend and former Columbia professor Mark Van Doren,

> I am tremendously busy with writing. Magazines are beginning to be after me, and I have to do a lot of judicious refusing. I can only write for magazines on condition that I keep myself in one field & on one plane—and the nearer it is to mystical theology the better. My superiors have more or less let me go off on my own & make all my own decisions as far as writing is concerned with the one exception—they won't let me give it up.[1]

At this point Merton had been a member of the monastic community at the Abbey of Gethsemani in rural Kentucky for almost six years, and up until the previous few months he had published nothing[2] as a monk but poetry,[3] though he had already written the

---

[1] Thomas Merton, *The Road to Joy: Letters to New and Old Friends*, ed. Robert E. Daggy (New York: Farrar, Straus & Giroux, 1989), 21.

[2] Two anonymous translations had appeared the previous year: *The Soul of the Apostolate*, by Jean-Baptiste Chautard (Trappist, KY: Abbey of Gethsemani, 1946), and *The Life and Kingdom of Jesus in Christian Souls*, by Saint John Eudes (New York: P. J. Kenedy & Sons, 1946).

[3] Merton had published three volumes of verse by this time: *Thirty Poems* (Norfolk, CT: New Directions, 1944); *A Man in the Divided Sea* (New York: New Directions, 1946); and *Figures for an Apocalypse* (New York: New Directions, 1947). Individual poems had appeared in *Catholic Art Quarterly*, *Chimera*, *The*

autobiography that would make him famous when it came out the following year,[4] along with various other prose works on monastic topics that appeared over the course of the next couple of years.[5] But between July 1947 and March 1950 he would publish eleven substantial articles for a general audience in various Catholic periodicals,[6] on topics related directly or indirectly to contemplation, with an additional short piece appearing in March 1952. Half of these articles appeared in the lay-edited magazine *The Commonweal* (as it was then called), where he had been publishing poetry since mid-1946; four pieces came out in rapid succession in the last six months of 1947, with the final two in late 1949 and early 1950. The other six appeared in five different publications—*Integrity*, *The Messenger of the Sacred Heart*, *The Dublin Review*, *Cross and Crown*, and *Action Now!*—between November 1947 and March 1952.

The earliest of these articles, "Poetry and the Contemplative Life," as its title suggests, explores the interface between the work of the literary artist and the vocation of the contemplative that continued to absorb Merton's attention in theory and in practice until the very end of his life. Two of the other *Commonweal* articles

---

Commonweal, *The New Yorker*, *Poetry*, *The Quarterly Review of Literature*, *Sewanee Review*, *Spirit*, *Tiger's Eye*, *Voices*, and *Western Review*.

[4] Thomas Merton, *The Seven Storey Mountain* (New York: Harcourt, Brace, 1948).

[5] Thomas Merton, *Cistercian Contemplatives: A Guide to Trappist Life* (Trappist, KY: Abbey of Gethsemani, 1948); Thomas Merton, *Exile Ends in Glory: The Life of a Trappistine, Mother M. Berchmans, O.C.S.O.* (Milwaukee: Bruce, 1948); Thomas Merton, *Guide to Cistercian Life* (Trappist, KY: Abbey of Gethsemani, 1948); Thomas Merton, *The Spirit of Simplicity* (Trappist, KY: Abbey of Gethsemani, 1948).

[6] Merton would also publish a rather technical five-part article on Saint Bernard and Saint John of the Cross in the official journal of the Cistercian Order during this period: Thomas Merton, "The Transforming Union in St. Bernard and St. John of the Cross," *Collectanea Ordinis Cisterciensium Reformatorum* 9, no. 2 (1948): 107–17; 9, no. 3 (1948): 210–23; 10, no. 1 (1949): 41–52; 10, no. 3 (1949): 353–61; 11, no. 1 (1950): 25–38; reprinted in Thomas Merton, *Thomas Merton on St. Bernard* (Kalamazoo, MI: Cistercian Publications, 1980), 159–226.

from 1947, "The Trappists Go to Utah" and "A Christmas Devotion," as well as "Death of a Trappist," which appeared in *Integrity* in November of that year, deal with mysticism only tangentially, the first and third addressed to the widespread fascination with and curiosity about the lives of those belonging to the strictest monastic order at the time established in the United States, while the Christmas article considers the meaning of the Incarnation from a perspective that differs radically from the usual focus on the crèche and on the coming of Christ as Savior and Redeemer.

The 1948 article in *The Messenger of the Sacred Heart*, entitled "A Trappist Speaks on People, Priests and Prayer," is addressed to an audience that would probably find the notion of contemplation exotic and alien to their own lives and thus emphasizes intercessory prayer, while the 1950 Lenten article "Self-Denial and the Christian," the last of the *Commonweal* pieces from this period, focuses more on the ascetic than the mystical dimension, though it affirms the continuity between these two phases of the spiritual life. The final "early essay" included here, "Christ Suffers Again," a brief piece that appeared in *Action Now!* in March 1952, emphasizes the paschal identification of the poor and oppressed with the crucified Christ and thus looks forward to Merton's more socially conscious writings of the last decade of his life.

The rest of the articles correspond closely to the description Merton gave to Van Doren of a concentration on "one field & on one plane—and the nearer it is to mystical theology the better." They are most akin in focus and tone to *The Ascent to Truth*,[7] Merton's most systematic attempt to develop a theology of the mystical life, on which he was working during this same period. In a February 15, 1949, journal entry, Merton writes of this project, which has not yet been given its final title:

> However, about *The Cloud and the Fire*, I have in mind something that needs to be done some day: the dogmatic essentials of mystical theology based on tradition, and delivered in the context and atmosphere of Scripture and the Liturgy. In other

---

[7] Thomas Merton, *The Ascent to Truth* (New York: Harcourt, Brace, 1951).

words a mystical theology that is not a mere catalog of "experiences," many of them outside the range of the ordinary economy of the Gifts, but a book that drinks contemplation *de fontibus Salvatoris* [from the wellspring of the Savior] and exploits all the mysticism there is in the Liturgy and in revelation: an *objective* mysticism, integrated with the common intellectual heritage of the Church as a whole and yet with its full subjective application to the experience of the actual or potential mystic, the concrete and individual contemplative. The contemplation of the Mystical Body in all its members. Reverend Father thought it was a good idea to work towards it and to take it step by step, getting the various parts up as magazine articles first of all.[8]

While the magazine articles were not incorporated *per se* into the book, they explore many of the same ideas and themes.

The third of Merton's four *Commonweal* articles of 1947, "Active and Contemplative Orders," first engages the issue of contemplation and its role as the foundation of authentic apostolic action, while his piece for the same journal almost two years later, "Is Mysticism Normal?," presents a nuanced positive answer to the title's question that both affirms the normative character of mysticism and explains its apparent rarity in the lives of the majority of Christians. Substantial articles in three other journals, one each for the years 1948–1950, develop further the basic positions found in the pair of *Commonweal* essays. "Contemplation in a Rocking Chair," published in the August 1948 issue of *Integrity*, critiques an attitude toward contemplation that tends to underplay the commitment required to remain open to the transforming power of God in prayer. "The Contemplative Life: Its Meaning and Necessity," which appeared in *The Dublin Review* in Winter 1949, addresses various stereotypes that keep Christians from recognizing the centrality of contemplation for the life of the church and the lives of individual members of the Mystical Body. Finally, "The

---

[8] Thomas Merton, *Entering the Silence: Becoming a Monk and Writer. Journals*, vol. 2: *1941–1952*, ed. Jonathan Montaldo (San Francisco: HarperCollins, 1996), 282–83.

Primacy of Contemplation," in the March 1950 issue of *Cross and Crown*, revisits issues first raised in "Active and Contemplative Orders" and restates Merton's basic position, as found in the title, in response to criticism of the earlier article. By March 1950, Merton had virtually stopped writing shorter articles and did not resume doing so regularly until late 1956.[9] Both his success and his struggles in book-length projects of the period no doubt played a significant role in this shift of focus: *The Seven Storey Mountain* and *Seeds of Contemplation*,[10] his book of meditations published the following year, made him a household name in Catholic circles and encouraged him to continue writing full-length works, while the difficulties he experienced in trying to bring to completion *The Ascent to Truth*, his most theologically complex work, preoccupied his attention around this time. But already in mid-1948 he had also been advised by Cistercian Vicar General Gabriel Sortais (soon to become Abbot General of the Order) not to become too committed to periodical publication. In an August 20, 1948, journal entry, Merton writes, "Dom Gabriel told me not to let myself get roped into any magazine as a *collaborateur*, i.e., not to get my name on the mast-head as a staff writer, and be slow to accept work. They are all commercial. They ruin you. Told me to refuse book-reviews except in exceptional cases."[11] By early 1952, as his godfather Ed Rice began planning

---

[9] Merton did contribute to two collections of essays in the early 1950s: an autobiographical piece entitled "The White Pebble" appeared in *Where I Found Christ*, ed. John A. O'Brien (Garden City, NY: Doubleday, 1950), 235–50 (also published in abbreviated form in *Sign* magazine in July 1950), and "St. John of the Cross" appeared in *Saints for Now*, ed. Clare Boothe Luce (New York: Sheed & Ward, 1952), 250–60. Both of these articles are now available in Thomas Merton, *Selected Essays*, ed. Patrick F. O'Connell (Maryknoll, NY: Orbis, 2013), 3–14, 15–22. Virtually all the rest of his prose in popular magazines from mid-1950 through late 1956 consisted in excerpts of material that had been or would be published in books (or, in the case of *The Seven Storey Mountain*, of unpublished portions of the manuscript that Merton's friend and correspondent Sr. Thérèse Lentfoehr had selected).

[10] Thomas Merton, *Seeds of Contemplation* (New York: New Directions, 1949).

[11] Merton, *Entering the Silence*, 226.

his photo-magazine *Jubilee*, Merton wrote to his friend Sr. Thérèse Lentfoehr, "I am supposed to have backed out of the magazine field altogether. The Abbot General definitely told me to keep my name off the masthead of any magazine—even as advisor."[12]

As early as September 1947, however, when only the first two *Commonweal* essays were in print, Merton was already thinking about gathering them together for a book, writing in his journal on September 25, "My heart burns in my side when I write about contemplation in an article or anywhere. . . . I don't feel these articles for *Commonweal* are useless, and they may make a book."[13] The idea is still on his mind in the spring of 1950 when he writes to his agent Naomi Burton on Holy Thursday about the possibility of James Laughlin of New Directions, which had issued *Seeds of Contemplation* and four volumes of Merton's verse,[14] publishing "the collection of articles, which will soon enough be big enough for a book. . . . The articles are solid enough."[15] By the end of the year he is mentioning "that collection of articles" in a December 21 letter to his other main publisher, Robert Giroux of Harcourt, Brace, and he brings it up again in letters of January 20 and February 4, 11, and 13, 1951.

The last of these letters refers to the publication of *The Ascent to Truth* and says that the book of essays "can follow later," but in fact he shelved the project indefinitely, and a volume containing these pieces never appeared. Consequently most of this material has remained virtually unknown to Merton readers and even to scholars, though the articles represent a significant component of Merton's writing career during the period that saw the publication of his autobiography, his ordination to the priesthood, and the beginning of his work as a teacher of the young monks and novices at the Abbey of Gethsemani. While not equal in importance or achievement to the major essays he wrote on a wide variety of

[12] Merton, *Road to Joy*, 210 (February 4, 1952).
[13] Merton, *Entering the Silence*, 122–23.
[14] *The Tears of the Blind Lions* had appeared in 1949.
[15] Thomas Merton, *Witness to Freedom: Letters in Times of Crisis*, ed. William H. Shannon (New York: Farrar, Straus & Giroux, 1994), 127.

topics in the final decade of his life,[16] this group of shorter writings documents Merton's early efforts to comprehend and explain the meaning of contemplation within and beyond monasticism and to bring a clearer and more accurate understanding of key elements of Cistercian life to American Catholics and others.

Thus the present volume is intended to realize at long last Merton's own original plan of publishing these essays as a group and so to make available a previously little-recognized and under-utilized resource for understanding and appreciating a crucial transitional phase in his life as both monk and writer. The essays are grouped into two parts—the first consisting of the six essays published in *The Commonweal*, the second of the six essays that appeared elsewhere—a division that allows the audience to read sequentially the pieces found in Merton's favorite outlet for his prose during this period and then to consider chronologically the expanded audience he sought to reach in the variety of publications and differing audiences of the remaining essays. Each of the essays is preceded by an introductory headnote providing whatever information is available on the circumstances of composition and publication along with brief indications of major points raised in that essay.

For the three essays that were reprinted in some form subsequent to their initial periodical publication, textual notes listing all variant readings are provided in Appendix 1. A second Appendix reprints the article "States of Life" by John Fearon, O.P., a critique published in *The Thomist* of Merton's *Commonweal* article "Active and Contemplative Orders," followed by Merton's own extensive journal comments on Fearon's article. Together with Merton's later article "The Primacy of Contemplation," these pieces provide comprehensive documentation of a controversy that left Merton himself both chastened and bemused.

Particular thanks are due to Peggy Fox, Anne McCormick, and Mary Somerville, trustees of The Thomas Merton Legacy Trust,

---

[16] For an overview of Merton's writings in this genre, see "Merton the Essayist," the Introduction to *Selected Essays*, ix–xviii.

for permission to publish this edition of Merton's early essays, and to Jonathan Montaldo, former director of the Thomas Merton Center at Bellarmine University and editor of numerous Merton works, including *Entering the Silence*, the second volume of Merton's journals, and *The Intimate Merton*,[17] for his gracious and insightful foreword to this volume.

[17] Thomas Merton, *The Intimate Merton: His Life from His Journals*, ed. Patrick Hart and Jonathan Montaldo (San Francisco: HarperCollins, 1999).

Part I

Articles from *The Commonweal*

Poetry and the Contemplative Life

On May 14, 1947, Thomas Merton wrote in his journal, "yesterday . . . I signed the contract for *Figures for an Apocalypse* with
New Directions and heard that Commonweal got the *imprimatur*
[ecclesiastical approval] on an article on Poetry and the Contemplative Life, which I rather wanted to get back from them, but they
want to print it" (*Entering the Silence*, 74). The article referred to
appeared in *The Commonweal* July 4, 1947, 280–86, and in slightly
revised form in Merton's third book of verse (93–111), mentioned
in the same journal entry. The text included in the present volume
draws on both versions of the essay: see Appendix 1 for a list of
variants and the choice of readings made in each case. The essay
consists of a lengthy introduction followed by a three-part central
section and a brief conclusion. Its introduction focuses on the
contemplative life as the normal culmination of spiritual development, though Merton argues that it remains a pure gift that
relatively few are ready to receive in their earthly lives. He then
turns to the relationship of contemplation and art, pointing out
first that contemplation has much to offer the poet and encouraging Catholic writers to lead lives of active contemplation that will
draw them closer to Christ through the disciplines of liturgy,
penance, prayer, and spiritual reading. He next makes the case
that the converse is also true, that poetry has something valuable
to offer contemplation because of the analogy between authentic
aesthetic experience and mystical prayer. But he also indicates
that beyond a certain point poetry and contemplation can begin
to pull in different directions: whereas the infused contemplative
experience is passive and receptive, allowing God to do his

3

transforming work within the soul, the artistic experience remains active and creative, interested in what happens within the artist, however significant it may be in itself, primarily as raw material for the art. In artistic activity the higher good risks being sacrificed for the lower, the perfecting of the soul for the perfecting of the work. Merton concludes that while poetry can be of great assistance during the early stages of contemplative life, to cling to artistic activity as one moves toward the higher levels of infused contemplation is to risk arresting further spiritual development. He does, however, leave some room for coexistence of the two: personal moral certainty or the desire of a religious superior that one should continue to write for the benefit of others could be a sign that in a particular case a "ruthless sacrifice" of one's art is not called for. Some comfort may be taken from the teaching of Saint Thomas Aquinas that sharing the fruits of contemplation is more meritorious than simply enjoying them oneself, and there is no one better prepared than the artist to articulate "what is essentially inexpressible." Already in the spring of 1950 Merton indicated an apparent dissatisfaction with the way the piece ends, writing to Naomi Burton that he "would rewrite the conclusion" if the article were to be reprinted in a collection of his essays (*Witness to Freedom*, 127). In 1958, once again in *Commonweal*, Merton published a revised version of this essay as "Poetry and Contemplation: A Reappraisal" (Oct. 24, 1958, 87–92), in which he presented a more capacious view of contemplation and a more flexible understanding of its relationship to artistic creativity (for a comparison of the two versions see Patrick F. O'Connell, "Poetry and Contemplation: The Evolution of Thomas Merton's Aesthetic," *The Merton Journal* 8, no. 1 [2001], 2–11). But the original version reprinted here remains a significant milestone in Merton's developing theory of art and a helpful guide to his personal struggles with his own practice as a poet in the late 1940s.

The term "contemplative life" is one that is much mistreated. It is more often used than defined, and that is why arguments about the respective merits of "active" and "contemplative" orders generally end nowhere. In the present article I am not talking about the contemplative orders, but about the contemplative life. It is a life that can be led and, in fact, must eventually be led by every good Christian. It is the life for which we were created, and which will eventually be our everlasting joy in heaven. By the grace of Christ we can begin to lead that life even on earth, and many in fact do so begin. Some of them are in cloisters, because the vows and rules of religious orders and congregations make the necessary work of preparation easy and, as it were, almost a matter of course. But many more "contemplatives" are out in the world. A lot of them may be found in places like Harlem and wherever people suffer, and perhaps many of these have never even heard the word "contemplative." And yet on the other hand, not all those who are in contemplative orders are contemplatives. Through their own fault they miss the end of their vocation.

The contemplative life is a life entirely occupied with God—with love and knowledge of God. It can be considered from three points of view, as it were in three degrees. There is first of all possible a kind of natural contemplation of God—that of the artist, the philosopher, and of the most advanced pagan religions. Then there is the contemplative life in the usual sense of the word: a life in which a baptized Christian, making full use of all the means which the Church puts at his disposal—Sacraments, Liturgy, penance, prayer, meditation, spiritual reading and so on—strives to conform his will with God's will and to see and love God in all things and thus to dispose himself for union with Him. This is *active* contemplation, in which grace indeed is the principle of all the supernatural value and ordination of our acts, but in which much of the initiative belongs to our own powers, prompted and sustained by grace. This form of the contemplative life prepares us for contemplation properly so called: the life of *infused* or *passive* or *mystical* contemplation.

Infused contemplation is nothing but the fullness of the Christian life—the flowering of grace and the gifts and beatitudes which perfect the work of the three theological virtues.

Far from being something esoteric and dangerous, infused contemplation is given us as the normal term of the Christian life even on earth. *Omnis qui ad Dominum convertitur contemplativam vitam desiderat* said Saint Gregory the Great, and he was using contemplation in our sense: to live on the desire of God alone; to have one's mind divested of all earthly things and united, in so far as human weakness permits, with Christ. And he adds that the contemplative life begins on earth in order to continue, more perfectly, in heaven. Saint Thomas echoed him with his famous phrase: *quaedam inchoatio beatitudinis*. Saint Bonaventure goes farther than any of the other Doctors of the Church in his insistence that all Christians should desire infused contemplation. And in his second conference on the Hexaemeron, applying Christ's words in Matthew xii, 42, he says that the Queen of the South who left her own land and traveled far to hear the wisdom of Solomon will rise up in judgment against our generation which refuses the treasures of infused wisdom, preferring the far lesser riches of worldly wisdom and philosophy.

Infused contemplation is an experimental knowledge of God's goodness "tasted" and "possessed" by a vital contact in the depths of the soul. By infused love, we are given an immediate grasp of God's own substance, and rest in the obscure and profound sense of His presence and transcendent actions within our inmost selves, yielding ourselves altogether to the work of His transforming Spirit.

Now whether we speak of contemplation as active or passive, one thing is evident: it brings us into the closest contact with the one subject matter that is truly worthy of a Christian poet: God as He is seen by faith, in revelation, or in the intimate experience of the soul illumined by the gifts of the Holy Ghost.

Consider, for instance, what a tremendous mine of literary inspiration is in the liturgical life. The liturgy itself contains the greatest literature, not only from Scripture, but from the genius of the Patristic and Middle Ages. The liturgy stands at the crossroads of the natural and supernatural lives, and exploits all the possibilities of both in order to bring out every possible meaning and implication that is in them with respect to our salvation and the praise of God. It surrounds those founts of all supernatural vitality, the Sacraments, with a music that is perfect in its dignity, and ceremonies that are most meaningful by reason of their tremendous dramatic simplicity, not to mention all the resources of pictorial and plastic art still unknown in this land which has never yet possessed a Chartres or an Assisi.

✠   ✠   ✠

The liturgy is, then, not only a school of literary taste and a mine of marvelous subjects, but it is infinitely more: it is a great sacramental built around the six Sacraments which surround the greatest Sacrament Who is Christ Himself dwelling among us even unto the consummation of the world.

Christ on the Cross is the fount of all art because He is the Word, the fount of all grace and wisdom. He is the center of everything, of the whole economy of the natural and the supernatural orders. Everything points to this anointed King of Creation Who is the splendor of the eternal light and the mirror of the Godhead without stain. He is the "image of the invisible God, the firstborn of every creature . . . in Him were all things created, by Him and in Him . . . He is before all and by Him all things consist . . . in Whom it hath pleased the Father that all things should dwell . . . for in Him dwelleth all the fullness of the Godhead corporeally," that in all things He may hold the primacy (Colossians, i and ii).

And yet Catholic poets and writers generally, although they might possess the key to these treasures through a love of Christ that would not shrink from the self-denial required to live a complete and integral Christian life in defiance of the standards of comfort-loving American materialism, prefer to struggle along in the wake of indifferent and mediocre secular models, singing the same old cracked tune that the Georgians inherited from Tennyson and Swinburne and of which even the children of our modern world have long since grown tired.

Of course, it is no wonder that we can't all live like a Saint John of the Cross. But we might at least *read* him! He is one of the greatest Catholic poets. How many Catholics have ever even heard of him? And yet every time you open a Catholic anthology you will come across something by Alexander Pope who was baptized a Catholic, indeed, and died one, but who *wrote* as a deist. Contemplation would at least open our eyes to the value of our own tradition, even if we did not have the courage to follow our models to the limit in order to come somewhere near the intensity and perfection of their writing.

No Christian poetry worthy of the name has been written by anyone who was not in some degree a contemplative. But that does not mean that every contemplative is necessarily a great poet. Poetry is an art, a natural skill, a virtue of the practical intellect, and no matter how great a subject we may have in the experience of infused contemplation, we will not be able to put it into words if we do not have the proper command of our medium. That is true. But let us assume that a man already has this natural gift. If the inspiration is helpless without a correspondingly effective technique, technique is barren without inspiration.

Christ is our inspiration, and Christ is at the center of the contemplative life. Therefore, it would seem fairly evident that the one thing that will most contribute to the perfection of Catholic literature in general and poetry in particular will be for our writers and poets to start leading lives of active contemplation. In other words, to lead the full Christian life in so far as they can in their state. That means not necessarily entering a monastery, but aspiring to perfection by the use of all the manifold means that the Church puts at our disposal. It means a solid integration of one's work and religion and family life and recreations in one vital harmonious unity with Christ at its center. The liturgical life is the most obvious example, but it is hard enough to find a parish where the liturgical life is anything more than a bare skeleton. Nevertheless, any man or woman in the world who wants to can make a very fair attempt at becoming an active contemplative and even dispose himself for the graces of infused prayer. And the best disposition is an efficacious desire to arrive at a deep and intimate and personal and loving knowledge of God through Christ.

If such a desire is efficacious, it will not shrink from penance and sacrifices; it will seek them. It will not be bored with prayer, but prayer will become the life of our soul, and we will be able to carry on affective prayer everywhere. We will read Scripture and above all the contemplative saints—John of the Cross, Teresa of

Avila, John Ruysbroeck, Bonaventure, Bernard and so on. And God will not make too many difficulties about giving us His wisdom. . . .

It is obvious, then, that contemplation has much to offer poetry. But can poetry offer anything, in return, to contemplation? Can the poetic sense help us towards infused contemplation, and, if so, how far along the way?

✠   ✠   ✠

We have said that the poetic sense may be a *remote* disposition for mystical prayer. This needs explanation. And the first thing that needs to be stressed is the essential dignity of esthetic experience. It is, in itself, a very high gift, though only in the natural order. It is a gift which very many people have never received, and which others, having received it, have allowed to spoil or become atrophied within them through neglect and misuse.

To many people, the enjoyment of art is nothing more than a sensible and emotional thrill. They look at a picture, and if it stimulates one or another of their sense-appetites they are pleased. On a hot day they like to look at a picture of mountains or the sea because it makes them feel cool. They like paintings of dogs that you could almost pat. But naturally they soon tire of art, under those circumstances. They turn aside to pat a real dog, or they go down the street to an air-conditioned movie, to give their senses another series of jolts. Obviously for such people art is not even a remote preparation for even the lowest degree of contemplation.

But a genuine esthetic experience is something which transcends not only the sensible order (in which, however, it has its beginning) but also that of reason itself. It is a supra-rational intuition of the latent perfection of things. Its immediacy outruns the speed of reasoning and leaves all analysis far behind. In the natural order, as Jacques Maritain has often insisted, it is an analogue of the mystical experience which it resembles and imitates from afar. Its mode of apprehension is that of "connaturality"—it reaches out to grasp the inner reality, the vital substance of its object, by a kind of affective identification of itself with it. It rests in the perfection of things by a kind of union which somewhat resembles the rest of the soul in its immediate affective contact with God in the obscurity of mystical prayer. A true artist can contemplate a picture for hours, and it is a real contemplation, too. So close is the resemblance between these two experiences that a poet like Blake could almost confuse the two and make them merge into one another as if they belonged to the same order of things. And yet there is an abyss between them.

Nowhere has this resemblance between the experiences of the artist and of the mystic been better treated than in the long and important article on "Art and Spirituality," by Fr. M. Leonard, S.J., in the "Dictionnaire de Spiritualité." This theologian stresses the dignity of the esthetic intuition practically to the limit. He gives it everything that it is ontologically able to stand. He insists that the highest experience of the artist penetrates not only beyond the sensible surface of things into their inmost reality, but even beyond that to God Himself. More than that, the analogy with mystical experience is deeper and closer still because, as he says, the intuition of the artist sets in motion the very same psychological processes which accompany infused contemplation. This would seem to be too much: but no, it is not. It fits in with the psychology of Saint Augustine and Saint Bonaventure and the latter's notion of contemplation *per speculum*, passing through the mirror of created things to God, even if that mirror may happen to be our own soul.

The Augustinian psychology, which forms the traditional substratum of Christian mystical theology, distinguishes between an *inferior* and *superior* soul. Of course, this is only a manner of speaking. There is only one soul, a simple spiritual substance, undivided and indivisible. And yet the soul in so far as it acts through its faculties, making decisions and practical judgments concerning temporal external things, is called "inferior." The "superior" soul is the same soul, but now considered as the principle or *actus primus* of these other diverse and multiple acts of the faculties which as it were flow from this inner principle. Only the superior soul is strictly the image of God within us. And if we are to contemplate God at all, this internal image must be re-formed by grace, and then we must enter within ourselves by recollection, withdrawing our faculties from external things into this inner sanctuary which is the substance of the soul itself. The majority of people, even those who possess the gift of sanctifying grace, never enter into this inward self, which is an abode of silence and peace and where the diversified activities of the intellect and will are collected, so to speak, into one intense and smooth and spiritualized activity which far exceeds in its fruitfulness the plodding efforts of reason working on external reality with its analyses and syllogisms.

✠   ✠   ✠

It is here that contemplation really begins. It is into this substance or "center" of the soul, when it is suitably purified of images and attachments to sensible things, that the obscure light of infused contemplation will be poured by God, giving us experimental contact with Himself without the medium of sense species, which are, in any case, utterly incapable of apprehending Him.

And yet even in the natural order, without attaining to God in us, the esthetic experience introduces us into this interior sanctuary of the soul and to its inexpressible simplicity and economy and energy and fruitfulness.

Obviously, then, when the natural contemplation of the artist or the metaphysician has already given a man a taste of the peaceful intoxication which is tasted in the supra-rational intuitions of this interior self, the way is already well prepared for infused contemplation. And if God should grant that grace, the person so favored will be much better prepared to recognize it, and to cooperate with God's action within him. And this, as a matter of fact, is a tremendous advantage. The artist, the poet, the metaphysician is, then, in some sense already naturally prepared and disposed to remove some of the principal obstacles to the light of infused contemplation. He will be less tempted than the ordinary man to reach out for sensible satisfactions and imaginable thrills. He will be more ready to keep himself detached from the level of feeling and emotionalism which so easily make the devotion of less wary souls degenerate into sentimentality. The mere fact of the artist's or poet's good taste, which should belong to him by virtue of his art, will help him to avoid some of the evils that tend to corrupt religious experience before it has a chance to take root and grow in the soul.

If only we realized how much the work of the Holy Ghost is impeded in our souls by our insatiable emotional vulgarity—a vulgarity which we innocently bring with us into the House of God and coddle next to our heart our whole life long, never suspecting that it is a dead and poisoned thing. And the saddest of all is that this domestic enemy is nourished and encouraged by so much of the so-called pious "art" that infects the atmosphere of the Church in so many quarters. If there were no other proof of the infinite patience of God with men, a very good one could be found in His toleration of the pictures that are painted of Him and of the noise that proceeds from musical instruments under the pretext of being in His "honor."

Mystical contemplation is absolutely beyond the reach of man's activity. There is nothing he can do to obtain it by himself. It is a pure gift of God. God gives it to whom He wills, when He wills, and in the way and degree in which He wills. By cooperating with the work of ordinary grace we can—and, if we really mean to love God, we must—constantly grow and progress in charity and union with Him by our good works. But no amount of generosity on our part, no amount of effort, no amount of sacrifice will necessarily and immediately gain us progress in mystical prayer. That is a work that must be done by God acting as the "principal agent" (the term is that of Saint John of the Cross). If He is the principal agent, there is another agent: ourselves. But our part is simply to consent and to receive, and all the rest that we can do amounts to the more or less negative task of avoiding the obstacles to God's action, and keeping our own selfishness and sensuality out of His way. Saint Bonaventure tells us in many places that prayer and ardent desire can persuade God to give us this gift, and that *"industria"* on our part can open the way for His action. The term *industria* stands for active purification, and Saint Bonaventure means, by that, precisely the same thing that Saint John of the Cross talks about all through the "Ascent of Mount Carmel," namely the voiding and emptying of the soul, clearing it of all images, all likenesses of and attachments to created things so that it may be clean and pure to receive the obscure light of God's own presence. The soul must be stripped of all its desires for natural satisfactions, no matter how high, how noble or how excellent in themselves. As long as it rests in creatures, it cannot possess God and be possessed by Him, for the love of the soul for creatures is darkness in the sight of God. If we love created things and depend on them and trust in them rather than in God, it will be once again a case of God's light shining in the darkness, "and the darkness did not comprehend it" (John i. 5).

There is no need to insist on this, since it is the common doctrine of Christian mystical theologians. The one big obstacle to "unitive" or "connatural" or "affective" knowledge of God by infused contemplation (the terms are those of Saint Thomas and his followers) is attachment to human reasoning and analysis and discourse that proceeds by abstraction from sense images, and by syllogizing, to conclusions. In other words, a man cannot at the same time fly in an airplane and walk along the ground. He must do one or the other. And if he insist on walking along the ground—all right, it is no sin. But it will take him much longer and cost him much more effort to get to his destination, and he will have a much more limited view of things along his way. And the even greater obstacle to union with God by pure and infused love, or wisdom, is love of one's own satisfactions, attachment to one's own pleasure, the desire to rest in one's own achievements and in the work of one's own powers and will. If God is to do the work of infusing contemplation into our souls, we must not be busy with our own natural activity, which, *ipso facto*, excludes and prevents this complete freedom of action which God demands in us. All He wants from the mystic is cooperation, peaceful consent, and a blind trust in Him: for all this time, since the soul does not act, it remains blind and in darkness, having no idea where it is going or what is being done, and tasting satisfaction that is, at first, extremely tenuous and ineffable and obscure. The reason is, of course, that the soul is not yet sufficiently spiritualized to be able to grasp and appreciate what is going on within it. It remains with nothing but the vaguest and most general sense that God is really and truly present and working there—a sense which is fraught with a greater certitude than anything it has ever experienced before. And yet if we stop to analyze the experience, or if we make a move to increase its intensity by a natural act, the whole thing will evade our grasp and we may lose it altogether.

☩   ☩   ☩

Now it is precisely here that the esthetic instinct changes its colors and, from being a precious gift becomes a *fatal handicap.* If the intuition of the poet naturally leads him into the inner sanctuary of his soul, it is for a special purpose in the natural order: when the poet enters into himself, it is in order to reflect upon his inspiration and to clothe it with a special and splendid form and then return to *display it to those outside.* And here the radical difference between the artist and the mystic begins to be seen. The artist enters into himself in order to *work.* For him, the "superior" soul is a forge where inspiration kindles a fire of white heat, a crucible for the transformation of natural images into new, created forms. But the mystic enters into himself, not in order to work but to pass through the center of his own soul and lose himself in the mystery and secrecy and infinite, transcendent reality of God living and working within him.

Consequently, if the mystic happens to be, at the same time, an artist, when prayer calls him within himself to the secrecy of God's presence, his art will be tempted to start working and producing and studying the "creative" possibilities of this experience. And therefore immediately the whole thing runs the risk of being frustrated and destroyed. The artist will be cheated of a gift of tremendous and supernatural worth, and be left with nothing— but the experience of an artist. And instead of passing through the sanctuary of his own soul into the abyss of the infinite actuality of God Himself, he will remain there a moment, only to emerge again into the exterior world of multiple created things whose variety once more dissipates his energies until they are lost in perplexity and dissatisfaction.

There is, therefore, a tremendous danger that one who has the natural gift of artistic intuition and creation will be constantly cheated of the infinitely superior gift of the union of the soul with God which surpasses all understanding. He may well receive the first taste of infused prayer, for, as Saint John of the Cross says, that is granted to relatively many souls, and often quite soon in their spiritual life, especially in a monastery: but, because of this tragic promethean tendency to exploit every experience as material for "creation" he may remain there all his life on the threshold, never entering in to the banquet, but always running back into the street to tell the passers by of the wonderful music he has heard coming from inside the palace of the King!

⚜   ⚜   ⚜

What, then, is the conclusion? That poetry can, indeed, help to bring us rapidly through that part of the journey to contemplation that is called active: but when we are entering the realm of true contemplation, where eternal happiness begins, it may turn around and bar our way.

In such an event, there is only one course for the poet to take, for his own individual sanctification: the *ruthless and complete sacrifice of his art*. This is the simplest and the safest and the most obvious way—and one which will only appall someone who does not realize the infinite distance between the gifts of nature and those of grace, between the natural and the supernatural order, time and eternity, man and God. For the esthetic experience, like everything else temporal, lasts a moment and passes away. Perhaps it enriches the soul with a fuller natural capacity for further experience of the same order—but all such experience will end at death though we will eventually get it back with our bodies. Mystical prayer, on the contrary, enriches man a hundredfold more both in time and in eternity. It purifies the soul and loads it with supernatural merits, enlarging man's powers and capacities to absorb the infinite rivers of light which will one day be his beatitude. More than anything else it forms Christ in the soul. We become the sons of God, says Saint Thomas (In Matth. v), in so far as we participate in the likeness of God's only-begotten and natural Son, Who is begotten Wisdom, *Sapientia genita*. And therefore by participating in the Gift of Wisdom man arrives at sonship of God. And Saint Bonaventure adds that wisdom (that is mystical contemplation) is the crowning of Christ's work in souls on earth. *Haec sapientia reddit hominem divinum et Christus venit hanc docere.* This wisdom makes man divine, and it is this that Christ came on earth to teach (Coll. ii in Hexaemeron).

The sacrifice of an art would seem small enough price to pay for this "pearl of great price." But there is a further complication, which we can only adumbrate, before closing this article. What if one is morally certain that God wills him to continue writing anyway? That is, what if one's religious superiors make it a matter of formal obedience to pursue one's art, for some special purpose like the good of souls? That will not take away distractions, or make God abrogate the laws of the spiritual life. But we can console ourselves with Saint Thomas Aquinas that it is more meritorious to share the fruits of contemplation with others than it is merely to enjoy them ourselves. And certainly, when it comes to communicating some idea of the delights of contemplation, the poet is, of all men, the one who is least at a loss for a means to express what is essentially inexpressible.

The Trappists Go to Utah

On August 8, 1947, Merton wrote a letter (unpublished) to C. G. Paulding, managing editor of *The Commonweal*, offering the magazine "a story that may interest the readers of *Commonweal*— an account of our recent foundation in Utah. It is based on information received from members of the pioneer group, and I thought an 'inside' story might be worth while. If you cannot find a place for it, do you have any idea where else I might try it? It would help our men considerably to have something known about their work out there." Five days later, he wrote Mr. Paulding again with revisions suggested by one of the Order's censors and instructions to "cut out the word 'grand' before solitude in the second from the last line. Grand is a silly word sometimes." *The Commonweal* accepted the article, which appeared on August 29, 1947, 470–73. Unlike Merton's previous *Commonweal* article, this one is largely journalistic reportage, relating details of the three-day journey by rail from Kentucky to the new Cistercian foundation in Utah—in the process correcting some of the misconceptions circulated in secular news articles—describing the "wild, lonely" setting of the ranch on a hilltop overlooking the Ogden valley where the monastery was to be built and providing details of the monks' initial process of settling in at what would be called Our Lady of the Holy Trinity Abbey. After commenting on the enthusiastic assistance of the bishop of Salt Lake City and his staff in making the new monastery possible in that predominantly Mormon state, Merton predicts that "the Cistercians will win the sincere admiration of many in Utah as they have everywhere else." He concludes by pointing out that while the monks'

17

"agricultural apostolate" will no doubt attract the widest attention, their primary purpose there as elsewhere is to live the full
contemplative life intrinsic to the Cistercian vocation. He also
suggests that this second recent foundation of Cistercian men,
along with the first American monastery of Cistercian women,
which was about to be formed in Massachusetts (Wrentham),
are signs of "the final perfecting and maturing of the Church in
America." In journal entries from November 10, 1946, through
August 3, 1947, Merton had traced the process of the Utah
foundation from the initial purchase of the land through the
community's early experiences there (*Entering the Silence*, 20, 22,
23, 25–26, 48, 72, 87–90, 92, 96), mentioning specifically in the last
of these entries a notebook that "Fr. Xystus . . . filled with writing," which "is being read in the refectory" and which evidently
served as a primary source for his own article. In the same entry
he mentions that he has "practically finished a special booklet on
our life" (*Cistercian Contemplatives*) being prepared as part of the
celebration of the one hundredth anniversary of the founding of
the Abbey of Gethsemani in 1848. This booklet included a brief
chapter entitled "Our Lady of The Most Holy Trinity" (33–36),
incorporating much of the same information as in the article
about the site and the initial process of the monks' settling in,
along with a page of photographs of the landscape and the monks
at work. A slightly updated account appeared the following year
in *The Waters of Siloe*, Merton's history of the Order (243–49),
which notes in its conclusion that the first Mass of the new community, celebrated on the train in St. Louis (the opening scene of
his article), took place on the same day as final Masses at the
Cistercian abbey of Our Lady of Consolation in China, which was
shut down by Communist authorities that day—a "providential"
concurrence that was not known at the time Merton wrote
his essay.

When the citizens of St. Louis went to breakfast on the seventh
of July, this year, they found strange headlines. In the middle of
the usual floods and politics and acts of violence was an item that
might almost have concerned ambassadors from Mars. It must
have made many good people uneasy to read the startling words:

"Monks in locked car in Station Yards." Pursuing the subject further, they discovered that the monks in question were the silent Trappists. (In secular newspapers Trappists always end up by being saddled with a "vow of silence.") The car had been there for some hours, and the monks were inside with the blinds down, and many curious people were on the outside in the hot sun, and one porter and three yard detectives were keeping the people on the outside from getting at the monks on the inside. Either that, or they were keeping the monks in the car from escaping. No one could be quite sure which. But in any case, the upshot of the whole affair was that the men inside that railway car were saying Mass.

That is more or less the way it is every time the Cistercians of the Strict Observance—which is their true name—get into the headlines. Newspapermen can never seem to figure them out, and with all their good will they invariably end up by printing something that makes the monks look like the most solemn idiots you ever imagined.

The truth about the men in that railway car is that they were very holy and very simple and very happy and very human men who were going calmly about a piece of work that had been assigned to them by obedience. Perhaps it may help a little to put some flesh and bones on the poor ghosts, and tell people what they were really doing.

There were thirty-five of them. Thirty-four were Trappist monks, brothers and novices from Gethsemani, Kentucky. The thirty-fifth was their Reverend Father Abbot, Dom Mary Frederic Dunne—the first native-born American who managed to survive the austerity of Cistercian life at Gethsemani, where he entered in 1894. He was taking this group of men to Huntsville, Utah, to make Gethsemani's second foundation in three years.

There is a story in that, too. In recent years, especially since the war, the growth of this ancient abbey (which celebrates its centenary next year) has been phenomenal. It is nothing unusual to see ex-service men lining up four and five at a time in the chapter room to exchange an "old man" of khaki for the white cloak of a choir novice or the brown cape of a brother. There has hardly been anywhere for them to sleep. Cubicles have been fixed up for them in every odd corner—and still they keep coming. Two world wars have taught America something about the value of asceticism, prayer, penance: and grace has given the young men of our nation something of a thirst for the knowledge of God that is to be had only by those who love Him and give themselves to Him alone.

Of the thirty-four Utah colonists, more than half were Trappists of less than six years' standing, many of these being war-veterans. Consequently it was a young and enthusiastic group that crowded that railway car, kneeling in the aisles while one monk held the *mensa* of a portable altar resting on two seats, and another held the chalice steady, and others took turns to offer the Sacrifice of Christ's Body and Blood in the yards of St. Louis's Union Station.

Every moment of the three days' journey was assigned, as far as possible, to some function prescribed in the Cistercian Usages. The monks recited the Canonical Office and the Little Office of the Blessed Virgin. They made their meditations and read the books they had brought with them. (One of their favorites, these days, is "The Spiritual Doctrine of Elizabeth of the Trinity.") They held their daily chapter with martyrology and all, even the Father Abbot's explanation of the Rule. The only thing omitted was the chapter of faults. The monks got up later than usual, remaining in their berths until four-thirty a.m.—but the reason for this was that they went to bed later at night. No sleeping was allowed outside the regular time, and the rule of silence was kept strictly as usual.

Of course, Cistercian silence is conditional. The Superior can always give permission to speak. But permission is not given at random, even on a train journey. At one point in the trip several of the monks were gathered around their Father Abbot, who had a map of the country they were going through, and they were discussing the landscape. One of the priests—a voluble little man from whom the rule of silence demands considerable self-control— was trying to inveigle permission to tell a funny story. He was consistently rebuffed. Finally he said meekly, but insistently: "Reverend Father, may I say something that has practical value?"

"Yes," said his Abbot, "go away and say three Our Fathers."

The newspaper statement that the Cistercian monks traveled three-quarters of the way across the continent "unseen and unseeing" with the blinds down all the way to Utah was too picturesque to be true. Trappists are, among other things, farmers. And they took a considerable interest in the corn that was growing in Missouri and the wheat that was being harvested in Kansas. But they are, above all, contemplatives: and the Rocky Mountains are nothing to be despised! They have something very eloquent to say about the God Whose power they reflect: and if Trappists did not have an ear to catch that message—who would there be to hear it?

The site of the new monastery is one of the most perfect settings for the contemplative life in the world. The monks have purchased a 1,640-acre ranch at the head of the Ogden Valley, and eighteen miles east of Ogden. It is reached by road through a long canyon carved out of the rock by the Ogden river. At some two thousand feet above Ogden itself, the valley broadens out and the Cistercians have settled in a mile-wide bowl among hills covered with sagebrush and ringed by high mountains which are several miles further away.

✠   ✠   ✠

When they arrived from Kentucky with its July heat and saw snow-covered Mount Ogden and Ben Lomond the monks began to realize that they had done some traveling! Of course, the summer sun can burn in Utah too, but it is a dry heat, and reports come in from the new monastery that work in the mountains is not unpleasant even when the temperature is high. Damp clothes dry out even before you change them. The contrast with Kentucky is striking. Here dry clothes get wet before you have had them on a minute.

The monks have settled in a wild, lonely spot. To the east of them is nothing but a wilderness without roads or farms. It is a paradise for hunters who, in the past, made the monks' ranch their base, and worked eastward from there. Deer come down to drink at one of the two plentiful springs on the Trappists' ranch, and about the only sound you hear in the valley is the howling of coyotes on the mountain side. At least, that was all you heard until the Cistercians set up their bell and began to ring it for Office and Mass.

It is something new indeed for the Rocky Mountains to hear a chapel bell call monks to choir in two o'clock in the morning, and later ring the consecration of a conventual Mass. And it was not without a certain exultation that the Cistercians bowed to the floor as the Body of Christ was raised above the altar for the first time in that lonely valley! For thousands of years those silent, arid rocks, magnificent in their stark beauty, have nevertheless been waiting for the coming of someone like these Trappists to make them complete. Contemplatives are chosen by God to be the voice of His whole creation, praising Him and adoring Him for the inanimate and brute beings that cannot praise Him, as well as for those who have reason but will not adore Him, or cannot find the time.

However, it must not be imagined that the Cistercians came to their new home and fell on their knees and remained in prayer for the rest of the week. When a monastery is founded things never seem to be that simple.

There were no dwellings on the property, but a contract had been made for six sections of war-service barracks that had been in use housing German and Italian prisoners during the war. These were to have been hauled to the ranch and set up and made ready in time for the arrival of the Trappists. Unfortunately, when they set foot on the soil of their new home in the early afternoon of July 10th the monks found only a part of the accommodations they had contracted for, and that part was cluttered with lumber and other materials. They cleared a way for themselves and Mass was said and they all broke their fast at about four in the afternoon, except for the Cellarer who was down in Ogden supervising the baggage that was still waiting to be picked up at the station. He came home at six p.m., hoping for Communion, but he had been forgotten in the confusion.

For the next few days the Trappists slept on the floor or on the predellas of altars in the barrack that was at once chapel, chapter room, refectory and dormitory, cloister, cellar, storeroom and workshop. The secular workmen who were supposed to be hauling the barracks to the site and helping the Trappists to get installed kept going off to do more lucrative jobs, and when the centenary of Brigham Young's arrival in Utah was celebrated barely two weeks after the Trappists came on the scene, the workmen made a long week end of it, but the monks were not sorry as they got a chance to have the Blessed Sacrament reserved during that time.

It was more than two weeks before everything was in order and it was possible to begin leading the regular life in its entirety, singing the office at the proper times and so on. But even now, and for many months and even years to come, manual labor will absorb much more of the monks' day than is usually prescribed.

There is a tremendous amount of work to be done before the new monastery of Our Lady of the Most Holy Trinity becomes a complete and self-sufficing Cistercian unit. The only thing the monks have is a ranch that grows plenty of hay and wheat. For the rest they must build an entire farm and monastery from the ground up. There is, above all, the problem of water. Utah is the land of "dry-farming" and irrigation. The best spring on the monks' land is plentiful indeed but it is a long distance from the good building sites and unless attempts to drill for a spring nearer at hand meet with success, the monks will be faced with the labor and expense of a mile-long pipeline. At present they walk the distance with milk cans every day. Several large reservoirs will have to be built, including tanks to catch and store the melting snow in spring. In Utah, every drop of water is worth money, and the monastery also possesses a handful of "water-right shares" which give it a claim on the organized and rationed supply.

The first question to be settled is that of a real home. The monks do not intend to spend the winter in their army huts if they can avoid it. A temporary monastery is already under construction. It will be made of metal "quonset huts," but will be one of the most elaborate "quonset" structures that has ever been attempted. It will contain everything that belongs to a Cistercian monastery, including Church and cloister and all the "regular" places as well as a guest house for visitors and retreatants. The two-story quadrangular building, centered upon a cloister garth or *préau*, will be spacious and solid since the monks may have to call it their home for twenty or twenty-five years to come.

A site for a permanent monastery has been tentatively chosen on a hilltop which commands a vast view of the valley and the mountains. Just as important as the temporary monastery will be the erection of barns and farm buildings and the formation of a herd of dairy cattle which will be the monastery's chief source of income. The monks will soon be manufacturing their famous "Port du Salut" cheese, although it is getting near the season of fasting, in which milk and cheese cease to play an important part in the monks' diet. Then there will have to be a garden and orchard, although it is improbable that they will attempt a vineyard. The land itself is extremely rich and promising. Digging the foundations of the temporary monastery they often went through ten or twelve feet of top-soil. A little irrigation will give them splendid crops of potatoes, beets, celery and all the staples of the Cistercian vegetarian diet.

The long Utah winters will present a problem; since there will be no trees to fell and no wood to chop the monks will have to find some indoor work to keep them busy when the snow lies deep on their valley. And it does lie deep, there, too. Last winter there were some two hundred inches of it, and beyond the hills, where there was twice that much, a skiing championship was held.

The Trappists have had a little difficulty in getting acclimatised. The journey and the revolution in their régime upset many stomachs and one of the Fathers had to go to the Benedictine nuns' hospital in Ogden with ulcers, which chose this inappropriate time to declare their presence. Many of the others kept getting violent nose-bleeds for the first few days, until they got used to the high altitude.

To compensate for these little trials they have had many consolations, the best of which was the ardent enthusiasm with which they were received not only by the Catholics—who are very much of a minority in Utah—but by non-Catholics as well. Bishop Duane Hunt of Salt Lake City worked hard to persuade Dom Frederic Dunne to make a foundation so far from home and under such numerous handicaps. The coming of the Cistercians is an answer to many fervent pleas and prayers, and consequently the Utah Catholics are delighted to see them. In fact, the Bishop spent the day at the monastery soon after the monks were installed and told them that they were his "only hope." His diocese is one of the largest in the United States and yet it barely occupies two pages in the Catholic Directory. Only half a dozen religious congregations and Orders are represented there by a mission or two and one or two schools and hospitals. Nevertheless the Church is gradually growing in Utah, which is seventy-five percent Mormon and in which all the Protestant sects have lost ground consistently since their establishment.

☩   ☩   ☩

How do the Mormons themselves feel about the Trappists? Individuals have proved themselves very courteous and friendly and no doubt the Cistercians will win the sincere admiration of many in Utah as they have everywhere else. However it is not likely that the Church of Jesus Christ of the Latter Day Saints will come out with an official public pronouncement welcoming the Trappists with open arms. Incidentally, when the monks packed up their personal belongings for the trip they seem to have found nothing available except cardboard boxes and containers which had previously served to ship whisky and which were obtained from neighboring stores in Kentucky. If the Mormons were paying close attention to the monks as they detrained in Ogden, they must have been very scandalized to see so many boxes labeled "Schenley's" and "Green River." Drinking liquor and coffee are two of the capital sins of Mormonism. However, when they find out that the monks do neither, the Latter Day Saints may feel a slight glow of official sympathy.

On the whole, the prospects of the new Cistercian foundation are very bright. They have a difficult task to perform, but everything is in their favor: and above all, they have an admirably chosen site.

Thanks to the untiring efforts of the late Monsignor Wilfrid J. Giroux of Ogden they secured what one of their friends described as the "best ranch in Utah." Monsignor Patrick Kennedy who has taken Monsignor Giroux's place in Ogden has also stepped into his rôle of the monks' best friend and has been joined by many others, both Catholic and non-Catholic, who have gone out of their way to surmise and cater to the Cistercians' every need.

✠   ✠   ✠

One thing, however, must be clear. The work which the monks have come to do in Utah is above all the work of contemplation. What will no doubt have the most forcible immediate effect on their neighbors will be their "agricultural apostolate," their transformation of an arid valley into an Eden of orchards and gardens. But this is only secondary. The Cistercian vocation is the work that excels all other works and that is performed in silence, in the depths of the soul. They have an apostolate, it is true, but it is an apostolate not of action but of union with God. Their apostolate is to fill themselves from the source of living waters, that grace may flow, through them, into the whole Church, and any rival enterprise that clouds the purity of heart on which this vocation depends, tends necessarily to diminish the efficacy of the monks' work in the Church. Their main concern must therefore always be to empty themselves of solicitude for created things in order to be filled with the obscure light and the dark fire of the Divinity of the Word, drawing them into Himself and uniting them to the Father by the bond of the Holy Spirit. This purity of heart which constitutes the monk's gift of himself to the action of God's love is the most powerful of means for bringing grace down upon the world.

This second Cistercian foundation in three years will soon be followed by the first establishment of Trappistine nuns in the United States. The site has already been selected in the Archdiocese of Boston and forty-nine applications have already been received. All these facts come together to point to the final perfecting and maturing of the Church in America. Without a full representation of the contemplative Orders, we cannot yet say, with complete confidence, that we have come of age. There are still one or two gaps, and perhaps the time has come when these too will be filled. Not the least significant date in the history of American Catholicism would be the foundation of a first American Charterhouse. Will the Carthusians come to our mountains and forests soon? The land is full of grand solitudes that await the semi-eremitical Orders. Whether they come to fill up the measure of the perfect age of Christ in us depends largely on our own bishops. We hope it will be soon.

Active and Contemplative Orders

Merton's third article in *The Commonweal* for 1947 appeared in the December 5 issue (192–96). In it Merton focuses on the apparently contradictory evaluations of the contemplative life found in Catholic teaching in general and in that of Thomas Aquinas in particular. Is contemplation to be regarded as more fruitful (Pope Pius XI) or more sterile (Saint Augustine) than the active life? If according to Saint Thomas the contemplative life is superior to the active, why does he teach that the so-called mixed life of preaching and teaching is to be considered superior to both of them? Merton's answer focuses on the traditional Thomistic idea of *contemplata tradere*, passing on the fruits of contemplation to others, as the essential element that explains the superiority of the mixed life, but he then goes on to reflect on what he sees as important implications of this teaching: first, that a life of teaching and preaching is to be preferred only in so far as it is based on and flows from an authentically contemplative experience of God; second, that sharing the fruits of contemplation is not to be understood as restricted to the activities of preaching and teaching but happens whenever a person is transformed by a profound encounter with Christ into an image of divine love and so radiates that love throughout the church and throughout the world; and finally, that this intrinsically contemplative transformation into Christ through participation in the paschal mystery is ultimately the vocation of all Christians, whether religious or laity, whether in orders classified as active, contemplative, or mixed. At the urging of Professor Francis X. Connolly of Fordham University, as Merton's November 12, 1949, letter to Sr. Thérèse Lentfoehr notes (see *Road to Joy*, 197), Merton incorporated this article in a radically abridged form—only about one-third of the original text is included—in the epilogue of his autobiography, *The Seven Storey Mountain* (414–19) (see Appendix 1 for a list of the differences in the two versions). In its original form, the article attracted the attention of a Dominican scholar, Fr. John Fearon, OP, who wrote a highly critical refutation of Merton's position in an article entitled "States of Life," published in *The Thomist* (12, no. 1 [1949]: 1–16). Fr. Fearon is dismissive, even contemptuous of Merton's arguments, claiming that he has failed to understand Saint Thomas's distinctions between active and contemplative states and active and contemplative lives, and that his assertion that all are called to a kind of "mixed life" of handing on the fruits of contemplation is confused and confusing. There is an undertone of defensiveness in Fr. Fearon's attack on what he evidently sees as a denigration of his own order and a misperception of the Thomistic arguments in its favor. In a succession of journal entries for January 22, 24, and 26, 1949 (*Entering the Silence*, 266–70; see also Merton's February 10, 1949, letter to Jacques Maritain [*Courage for Truth*, 23–24]), Merton admits the validity of some of Fearon's criticisms but points out that he was approaching the issue not as a juridical question or a matter of abstract theory, nor as a systematic theological analysis of the text of Aquinas, but in terms of its concrete application to the lives of Christians in general, and that he was drawing not only on Saint Thomas but also on Saint Bonaventure (as well as on Saint John of the Cross) to make his case. If Merton has missed some of Thomas's points, Fearon's unsympathetic reading has certainly missed some of Merton's—has "got it all distorted," as Merton himself puts it (see Appendix 2 for Fearon's article and Merton's journal entries in response).

There are paradoxes in the history of Christian spirituality and not the least of them is the apparent contradiction in the way the Fathers and modern popes have regarded the relation between the active and contemplative lives. Saint Augustine and Saint Gregory lamented the "sterility" of contemplation, which was in itself, as they admitted, superior to action. Yet Pope Pius XI came out in the constitution "Umbratilem" with the clear statement that the contemplative life was *much more* fruitful for the Church (*multo plus ad Ecclesiae incrementa et humani generis salutem conferre . . .*) than the activity of teaching and preaching. What is all the more surprising to a superficial observer is the fact that such a pronouncement should belong to our energetic times. You would have sooner attributed the thought to Saint Augustine and left Pius XI to worry about *"Rachel pulchra et infecunda"* the symbol of the fruitless contemplative vocation. Of course the Holy Father's purpose is quite evident once you note that he refers to Leo XIII's letter *"Testem benevolentiae"* as a prelude to his pronouncement. That letter, you remember, was addressed to Cardinal Gibbons, and some people are still touchy about the whole affair.

There is no need to be touchy about it. No such letter would be addressed, even by mistake, to us today. America is discovering the contemplative life. The discovery is slow in coming, perhaps. Our publishers are still very timid about putting out books that go very far into the interior life, but if they want to find out how misplaced are their fears let them consider the interest non-Catholics are showing in Saint John of the Cross (about whom there was recently an article in *Horizon*—a London magazine with intellectual pretensions) or let them remember that monasteries and booksellers who have been forced, by the demand, to reprint spiritual classics on their own initiative, have not suffered from it. The Trappists at Gethsemani, Kentucky, have had no trouble disposing of nearly ten thousand copies of a new translation of the "Soul of the Apostolate" in one year *without advertising*, and without the assistance of a corps of salesmen.

Then of course there is the increase of contemplative vocations.

All this invites us to reconsider a question that is by no means new, although perhaps it needs to be looked at in a new light. The argument "action vs. contemplation" goes back to the earliest days of the Church and it is not something that is so speculative that it has not many practical consequences that are vitally important to everyone.

Saint Thomas gave a classical summary of the whole thing in the *Summa Theologica*. But the trouble is, he gave us *two* classical summaries. And on the surface it is rather hard to reconcile them. They are both in the *Secunda Secundae* of the *Summa*. The substance of Question 188, article 6, has become quite familiar, at least in a garbled form. Practically anyone who realizes the existence of the debate can tell you that Saint Thomas taught that there were three vocations: that to the active life, that to the contemplative, and a third to the mixture of both, and that this last is superior to the other two. The mixed life is, of course, the vocation of Saint Thomas's own order, the Friars Preachers.

Not so many will be able to confuse you by contrasting this question with one which comes just a little ahead of it—one hundred and eighty-two. There Saint Thomas comes out flatly with a pronouncement no less uncompromising than the one we read from "Umbratilem." *Vita contemplativa*, he remarks, *simpliciter est melior quam activa* (the contemplative life in itself, by its very nature, is superior to the active life). What is more, he proves it by natural reason in arguments from a pagan philosopher—Aristotle. That is how esoteric the question is! Later on he gives his strongest argument in distinctly Christian terms. The contemplative life directly and immediately occupies itself with the love of God, than which there is no act more perfect or more meritorious. Indeed that love is the root of all merit. When you consider the effect of individual merit upon the vitality of other members of the Mystical Body it is evident that there is nothing sterile about contemplation. On the contrary Saint Thomas's treatment of it in this question shows that the contemplative life establishes a man in the very heart of all spiritual fecundity.

When he admits that the active life *can* be more perfect under certain circumstances, accidentally, he hedges his statement in with half a dozen qualifications of a strictness that greatly enhances what he has already said about contemplation. First, activity will only be more perfect than the joy and rest of contemplation if it is undertaken as the result of an overflow of love for God (*propter abundantiam divini amoris*) in order to fulfill His will. It is not to be continuous, only the answer to a temporary emergency. It is purely for God's glory, and it does not dispense us from contemplation. It is an added obligation, and we must return as soon as we morally can to the powerful and fruitful silence of recollection that disposes our souls for divine union.

When you see all this lined up in front of you, you turn back to Question one eighty-eight and readjust your spectacles. How can the two questions be made to fit together?

The only way to see clearly through the apparent contradiction is to weigh the words of the famous distinction of the three kinds of religious vocations by the balance of traditional teaching as well as Saint Thomas's own doctrine as we have just expressed it.

In Saint Thomas's time the "active life" had not quite crystallized out into its modern meaning. Today the "active life" means technically a vocation to some external works of charity or mercy for the good of others. But the Fathers are apt to make use of it as meaning the activity required for the practice of any virtue and anyone who is in the purgative or illuminative ways will then be leading an active life even though he were to be cloistered or lost in the depths of the desert. Ordinarily, of course, works of mercy would be included among such acts of virtue. Saint Thomas uses the term in both these different senses without giving any warning when he is about to make the change. Now when he speaks of the three kinds of vocation he clearly means the active life in the modern sense—a vocation to the service of other people. But nevertheless his threefold division presupposes a hidden use of the ancient meaning. When he ranks the three vocations in their order of dignity with the teaching Orders at the top, the contemplative Orders in the middle and the purely active Orders at the bottom of the scale he was obviously thinking of the traditional conception of the degrees of perfection that you will find so explicitly in Saint Augustine or Saint Bernard: first comes the active life (practice of virtues, mortification, charity) which prepares us for contemplation. Contemplation means rest, suspension of activity, withdrawal into the mysterious interior solitude in which the soul is absorbed in the immense and fruitful silence of God and learns something of the secret of His perfections less by seeing than by fruitive love.

Yet to stop here would be to fall short of perfection. According to Saint Bernard of Clairvaux it is the comparatively weak soul that arrives at contemplation but does not overflow with a love that must communicate what it knows of God to other men (Serm. 90 de Diversis). For all the great Christian mystics without exception, Saint Bernard, Saint Gregory, Saint Theresa, Saint John of the Cross, Blessed John Ruysbroeck, Saint Bonaventure, the peak of the mystical life is a marriage of the soul with God which gives the saints a miraculous power, a smooth and tireless energy in working for God and for souls which bears fruits in the sanctity of thousands and changes the course of religious and even secular history.

With this in mind, Saint Thomas could not fail to give the highest place to a vocation which, in his eyes, seemed destined to lead men to such a height of contemplation that the soul must overflow and communicate its secrets to the world.

Unfortunately all this is by no means obvious in the text of that particular article (Q. 188, A. 6). In fact, taken by itself, the bare statement "the religious institutes which are ordered to the work of preaching and teaching hold the highest rank in religion" is, frankly, misleading. It conjures up nothing more than a mental image of some pious and industrious clerics bustling from the library to the classroom. If it meant no more than this the solution would be hardly comprehensible to a Christian. Yet the tragedy is that many—including members of those "mixed" Orders—cannot find in it any deeper significance. If you can give a half-way intelligent lecture applying some thoughts from scholastic philosophy to the social situation, that alone places you very near the summit of perfection. . . .

☧   ☧   ☧

No, we must turn back the pages to those flaming words which lay down the conditions under which it is valid to leave contemplation for action. First of all *propter abundantiam divini amoris*. The life of these mixed Orders is to be rated above that of the pure contemplatives only on the supposition that their love is *so much more vehement, so much more abundant* that it has to pour itself out in teaching and preaching.

In other words Saint Thomas is here teaching us that the so-called mixed vocation can only be superior to the contemplative vocation if it is itself *more contemplative*. This conclusion is inescapable. It imposes a tremendous obligation. Saint Thomas is really saying that the Dominican, the Franciscan, the Carmelite must be super-contemplatives. Either that or he is contradicting everything he said about the superiority of the contemplative life in Question one eighty-two.

Therefore it will readily be seen that the serene sentence of the Angelic Doctor that "it is better to pass on to others the fruits of contemplation (*contemplata aliis tradere*) than merely to contemplate and nothing else" has a very serious catch to it. The Orders that are dedicated to the teaching vocation must necessarily build their houses in or near towns and live in contact with the busy and violent—and vicious world. Yet they have this obligation to be so filled with the infused wisdom that teaches us the secrets of Divine Love in contemplation that they will overflow and teach that love to the world. But the indispensable condition for the contemplative life is at least some measure of silence and solitude and withdrawal from the world.

The so-called "mixed" Orders have always realized this and the Carmelites, for instance, have never considered a province complete unless it included several "deserts"—monasteries hidden in the mountains where the Fathers could retire to hermitages and live alone with God. After all, how can one fulfill a vocation to pass on the fruits of contemplation to others if he himself has no contemplation and no fruits?

Whether the "mixed" Orders today in America are actually as contemplative as this program would demand is a question the author of this article has no way of answering. But at any rate it seems that most of them have reached, in practice, a sort of compromise to get out of the difficulty. They divide up their duties between their nuns and their priests. The nuns live in cloisters and do the contemplating and the priests live in colleges and cities and do the teaching and preaching. In the light of *"Umbratilem"* and the doctrine of the Mystical Body this solution is at least possible, if conditions leave them with no other way out. Saint

Thomas, however, envisaged a program that was far more complete and satisfactory, for the individual and for the Church! But what about the contemplative Orders? Their rules and usages at least grant them all they need to dispose themselves for contemplation and if their members do not reach it, it is at least not because of any difficulty inherent in their actual way of life. Granting that they are, or can be, as contemplative as they were meant to be by their founders: are they anything else?

✠   ✠   ✠

The fact is, there does not exist any such thing as a purely contemplative Order of men—an Order which does not have, somewhere in its constitution, the note of *contemplata tradere.* The Carthusians, with all their elaborate efforts to preserve the silence and solitude of the hermit's life in their monasteries, definitely wrote into their original "Customs" the characteristic labor of copying manuscripts and writing books in order that they might preach to the world by their pen even though their tongues were silent.

The Cistercians had no such legislation, and they even enacted statutes to limit the production of books and to forbid poetry altogether. Nevertheless they produced a school of mystical theologians which, as Dom Berlière says, represents the finest flower of Benedictine spirituality. We have seen what Saint Bernard, the head of that school, had to say on the subject, and in any case even if the Cistercians never wrote anything to pass on the fruit of their contemplation to the Church at large, *contemplata tradere* would always be an essential element in Cistercian life to the extent that the abbot and those charged with the direction of souls would always be obliged to feed the rest of the monks with the good bread of mystical theology as it came forth in smoking hot loaves from the oven of contemplation. This was what Saint Bernard told the learned cleric of York, Henry Murdach, to lure him from his books into the woods where the beeches and elms had taught the Abbot of Clairvaux all his wisdom.

And these "purely active" Orders, what about them? Do any such things exist? The Little Sisters of the Poor, the nursing sisterhoods cannot truly fulfill their vocations unless there is something of that *contemplata tradere*, the sharing of the fruits of contemplation. Even the active vocation is sterile without an interior life, and, indeed, a deep interior life.

The truth is, in any kind of a religious Order there is not only the possibility but even in some sense the obligation of leading, at least to some extent, the highest of all lives—contemplation, and the sharing of its fruits with others. Saint Thomas's principle stands firm: the greatest perfection is *contemplata tradere*. But that does not oblige us to restrict this vocation, as he does, to the teaching Orders. They only happen to be the ones that seem to be best equipped to pass on the knowledge of God acquired by loving Him—if they have acquired that knowledge in contemplation. Yet others may perhaps be better placed for acquiring it.

In any case, there are many different ways of sharing the fruits of contemplation with others. You don't have to write books or make speeches. You don't have to have direct contact with souls in the confessional. Prayer can do the work wonderfully well, and indeed the fire of contemplation has a tendency to spread of itself throughout the Church and vivify all the members of Christ in secret without any conscious act on the part of the contemplative. But if you argue that Saint Thomas's context limits us at least to some sort of visible and natural communication with our fellow men (though it is hard to see why this should be so) nevertheless even in that event there exists a far more powerful means of sharing the mystical and experimental knowledge of God.

If we turn to the pages of Saint Bonaventure's *Itinerarium* we will find what is perhaps the best description ever written of this highest of all vocations. It is a description which the Seraphic Doctor himself learned on retreat and in solitude on Mount Alvernia. Praying in the same lonely spot where the great founder of his Order, Saint Francis of Assisi, had had the wounds of Christ burned into his hands and feet and side, Saint Bonaventure saw, by the light of a supernatural intuition, the full meaning of this tremendous event in the history of the Church. "There," he says,

"Saint Francis 'passed over into God' (*in Deum transiit*) in the ecstasy (*excessus*) of contemplation and thus he was set up as an example of perfect contemplation just as he had previously been an example of perfection in the active life in order that God, through him, might draw all truly spiritual men to this kind of 'passing over' (*transitus*) and ecstasy, *less by word than by example*" (Itin, vii. 3).

✠   ✠   ✠

Here is the clear and true meaning of *contemplata tradere*, expressed without equivocation by one who had lived that life to the full. It is the vocation to transforming union, to the very height of the mystical life and of mystical experience, to the very transformation into Christ that Christ living in us and directing all our actions might Himself draw men to desire and seek that same exalted union because of the joy and the sanctity and the supernatural vitality radiated by our example—or rather because of the secret influence of Christ living within us in complete possession of our souls.

And notice the tremendously significant fact that the Seraphic Doctor makes no divisions and distinctions: Christ imprinted His own image upon Saint Francis in order to draw not some men, not a few privileged souls, but *all* truly spiritual men to the perfection of contemplation which is nothing else but the perfection of love. Once they have reached these heights they will draw others to them in their turn. Thus all men are called to become fused into one spirit with Christ in the furnace of contemplation and then go forth and cast upon the earth that same fire which Christ wills to see enkindled.

This means, in practice, that there is only one vocation. Whether you teach or live in the cloister or nurse the sick, whether you are in religion or out of it, no matter who you are or what you are, you are called to the summit of perfection: you are called to be a contemplative and to pass the fruits of your contemplation on to others. And if you cannot do so by word, then by example.

Yet if this sublime fire of infused love burns in your soul, it will inevitably send forth throughout the Church and the world an influence more tremendous than could be estimated by the radius reached by words or by example. Saint John of the Cross writes: "A very little of this pure love is more precious in the sight of God and of *greater profit to the Church*, even though the soul appear to be doing nothing, than are all other works put together" (Spiritual Canticle, b, xxix, 2).

There are degrees and varieties in this perfection to which you are called, but these degrees do not depend on the means you have at your disposal for preaching divine union. On the contrary they are measured by the perfection of that union itself. You will most perfectly fulfill this great vocation not by being a great teacher or a great scholar but by being a great saint, and sanctity means perfect love of God. The teaching, the exterior works are only accidental. To make them the principal thing is to doom yourself to failure because that will lead you in the wrong direction: it will make you aim at the riches of knowledge rather than the spiritual poverty of the contemplative which is the indispensable prerequisite for acquiring the wisdom that is born of Christ's love.

A Christmas Devotion

This essay, which appeared in *The Commonweal* December 26, 1947, 270–72, three weeks after the previous article, initially seems to be the most dated of any of these early pieces, and in some ways it certainly is. Merton's assertion that Jesus was aware from the moment of his conception of his divine identity is simply impossible to reconcile with any contemporary understanding of Jesus' full humanity, which means his full participation in the normal processes and stages of physical and psychological development. Merton's intent is to stress that it was a man, a human being, who knew this, but it is that very humanity that is rendered problematic by the claim to omniscience being made not simply for a newborn but for a not-yet-fetus. But the interest and enduring significance of the article lie elsewhere, as the earliest published articulation of what Merton calls in a journal entry of the previous month (November 10, 1947) the "great Scotist doctrine" of "the absolute primacy of Christ" (*Entering the Silence*, 132), that is, the teaching of the great medieval Franciscan theologian Duns Scotus that the incarnation of the Word was not contingent on the Fall but was, and would have been, even had there been no original sin, the essential purpose and culmination of creation (for Merton and Scotus see the fine article by Daniel Horan, OFM: "Thomas Merton the 'Dunce': Identity, Incarnation, and the Not-so-Subtle Influence of John Duns Scotus," *Cistercian Studies Quarterly* 47.2 [2012]: 149–75). This belief that "Christ was promised first without scars," as Merton puts it in his 1949 poem "Dry Places" (*Tears of the Blind Lions*, 26 [l. 35]), is most memorably expressed in "The General Dance," the final chapter of *New Seeds of Contemplation*, where Merton writes, "The Lord made the world and made man in order that He Himself might descend into the world, that He Himself might become Man" (290). This same teaching, rooted particularly in the hymn found in Colossians 1:15-20, is the central point of this "Christmas Devotion," in which sinful humanity's primary perception of Christ "as a Savior and a Redeemer . . . a Messiah Who has come to deliver us from our-selves and give us peace" is juxtaposed to and contrasted with Christ's own self-understanding as "the reason why the world and the universe and all the living things and the men and the angels and all mighty spirits had been created." Whether this was indeed how Jesus in his own lifetime (much less in his mother's womb) perceived his identity and vocation, as Merton claims at this point, is much less significant than whether this magnificent vision of the cosmic Christ provides a deeper and richer Chris-tology than the alternative theory, as Merton would continue to suggest long after he had left behind the more theologically naïve aspects of his Christmas reflections here.

It is a terrible thing, that no one of us should realize what it means that there has been a Christmas in our world.

Yet some of us will, perhaps, say: "We know what it is all about. Christ is born."

"So Christ is born! And what does that mean?"

"It means we are redeemed; it means we are saved."

"Is that all?"

"Christ is born! We are going to go to heaven!" And I say to you, it is a terrible thing that none of us should be able to realize what it means, that there has been a Christmas in our world.

✠   ✠   ✠

Is this something that happens in every man's childhood? It hap-pened in mine. Yours too, I suppose. One day (which was almost certainly not Christmas) without any apparent reason or occasion, you suddenly became conscious of who you were. Your identity came out like an image on a negative, and it was real with a new and unfamiliar kind of reality that was realer than anything you knew.

It was something you felt to be too important to tell anybody, so important that it was impossible to explain. . . .

You had discovered that you were a person. You knew who you were.

There was once conceived a Man to Whom this happened at the first second when He came into existence.

A human Soul, a will capable of unimaginably great love and a mind wide enough to take in infinity: a soul, mind and will, which had, a moment before, been nothing, had not existed, came into being because in the heart of a girl an almost unspoken assent was given to a movement of great grace.

And in the fraction of a second in which this Soul, in its Flesh, began to exist, the Man Who was so conceived was at once awake and saw, not vaguely, not in mystery, not with surmise or question, but saw clearly, and fully, and without being dazzled or frightened—saw Who He was.

He saw Who He was, because when He awoke out of nothingness He was gazing, with His whole Intellect into the Face of the Infinite Truth Who was at the same time His Father and Himself.

This Man, Who had never before existed, and had just begun to exist, saw, realized, fully grasped the meaning not of the words "I exist, I am myself," but:

"I am God!"

That does not shake you? You can consider that proposition, and you are still conscious? That a Man should come into existence and at once fully comprehend, without a shadow of the slightest fear of any uncertitude, that He is God—this does not surprise you?

Perhaps you are thinking: It was not a surprise to Him, not even a discovery. He had known that forever. He was the Word.

You have not quite grasped the statement.

It was a *Man* that knew this thing, a Man's mind, a *human* intellect, a *human* soul, a soul that had not existed until that moment, a soul as created and as independent as your soul or mine, as human as yours or mine, with all the autonomous consciousness of an individual man who knows and loves and knows that he knows and loves, and is aware of himself as distinct from every other man.

It was not the Person of the Word that experienced what I have just said, but the human soul of Christ. And the Person of the Word has no intellect of His own as Word: His Divine Intellect is One with that of the Father and the Holy Ghost.

It was not the Word realizing that He was the Word but Christ's human soul realizing in the light of His own Divinity:

"I, an individual Man, distinct from all the other men who have been born and ever shall be born, *I am God!*"

And yet that proposition does not begin to tell us anything about what the soul of Christ saw and realized when He came into being and knew His own identity.

☦   ☦   ☦

There is a tremendous silence peculiar to victory.

It belongs to nothing else: only to victory.

It is so profound that it comprehends, absorbs, penetrates everything. The battle is all over. The horrible tornado of noise is all over. The killing has all stopped. Silence. Everything relaxes.

The quiet sinks into your muscles, seeps right through you, and slowly, sweetly, mightily illuminates, enriches the mind and pacifies the will, and embraces all the being that is yourself with a splendid calm. . . .

Take the Book of Psalms and read the second one in the book.

"Why have the gentiles raged, and the people devised vain things?

"The kings of the earth stood up and the princes met together against the Lord and against His Christ. Let us break their bonds asunder and let us cast away their yoke from us. He that dwelleth in heaven shall laugh at them: and the Lord shall deride them. Then shall He speak to them in His anger and trouble them in His rage. . . ."

Victory. Silence.

And out of the unfathomable deeps of the light of the heart of that silence the calm voice of everlasting Certitude:

"The Lord hath said to Me: *Thou Art My Son*, This day have I begotten Thee . . ."

✠   ✠   ✠

You know well enough what it is to love your friends. Their joy becomes your joy because you are anointed with gladness at the mere thought of the things that have enriched your friend's soul. To think how happy your friends are (when they are happy) is enough to make you happy all day long.

It is enough to love Christ, and to realize what was in the soul of Christ from the first moment that He began to be Christ—this, I say, is enough to make you happy forever. Only realize, and remember it. You will never know sorrow.

In a sense, that will be the best thing in heaven: realizing the glory of Christ's recognition of Who He Is. And that is a safe statement, because in this mystery most of all will we come somewhere near understanding the fullness of the infinite depths of the nature and essence of God Who is Love.

But we have not yet really said what that realization was.

We have put what Christ saw into the words "I am God." Translated, that means "I am everything." But that is not enough, and it is so inadequate that it gives a completely false idea.

Here is the true idea, and the one which alone really opens to us the way to enter into Christ's joy.

What He realized, on realizing Who He was, was not merely: "I am everything," but "*I have received* everything." *Omnia mihi tradita sunt.* "All things are delivered to Me and no one knoweth the Son but the Father: neither doth anyone know the Father but the Son, and he to whom it shall please the Son to reveal Him."

This is the thing Christ saw in that first moment of profound silence and which He contemplated in the solitude of His infinitely deep love all His days on earth, and which He contemplates in heaven, and in our tabernacles, at this hour.

From the soundless depths of the infinite Godhead into the depths and roots of His human soul and human being came not only creation and sustenance and assistance and all given power but His human being existed and subsisted in a Divine Person, so that His being was the Being of God and His acts were attributed to the Word of God, His love was God's love and His vision was God's vision, and all this was His by the gift and the eternal decree of the inconceivable, immense Love Who is God.

We who are little and weak, we who are straw men, we cannot think of the greatest experiences of life without seeing everything through the cloud of a fervid excitement. Love is too much for us. God is too much for us. His glory is apt to carry us away, sweep us out of ourselves. We lose all understanding in agitation and feeling and excitement.

With Christ it was not so.

You want to understand what is glory? The glory of God?

His soul embodied the philosopher's definition: *clara cognitio cum laude*—clear knowledge full of praise. For Christ's soul, from that first moment, was all clarity, all peace, all magnificent and luminous silence and all praise and in the first glance of His Man's life He did not fear to look straight, or to open to God His Heart's Love and receive the Love of God in one draught, in one tremendous breath!

And in that instant He saw—as He afterwards taught Duns Scotus to see, the He, Christ, this Man, this perfect Soul, this Sacred Heart, he was the reason why the world and the universe and all the living things and the men and the angels and all mighty spirits had been created. He was their Head, the Head of men and angels. He was their life, their salvation, their very reason for existence.

He saw that God, Who from all eternity loved Himself for the sake of His own perfect Love, wanted to share His Love with someone outside Himself, other than Himself. He willed to see His own Joy exulting in a will, an intellect other than His own and as perfectly as in His own. And instead of choosing an angelic spirit to receive this gift of Himself, He had chosen the humblest of the rational natures and united it to Himself in unity of Person, in order that His own magnificent Love might be the more exultant and exalted!

And the Christ Who came into being at that fraction of a second and realized Who He was and what was His immense dignity: He it was Who came into existence and looked, without fear or excitement, full into the face of the truth: *"I am that Man. I am the Christ. I am God."*

🕈   🕈   🕈

We who are men and are born into a world full of wars and sufferings which are the fruit of our own sins, we naturally look at the Incarnation first of all from our point of view. Before everything else we see that the Child Christ is born to us as a Savior and a Redeemer. We lift up our heads in the middle of our grief and look upon a Messiah Who has come to deliver us from ourselves and give us peace, peace in our hearts and joy.

But the Christ Who is born to us is not thinking most of all of our sins or of His Cross. These only enter into His vision in an incidental way, *per accidens.*

Realizing Who He is, contemplating the terrific Love that has given Him a Divine Existence, He instantly does the one thing that He was brought into the world to do: He answers the gift of God to Himself by the entire offering of Himself to God.

He would have done the same thing if there had never been a sin in the world. He was born for one thing only: to give God perfect glory by His love, and to bring all rational and spiritual beings into participation of His own Love of God. And thus the whole universe would give God glory in Christ.

At the first moment of His Incarnation, in the clarity of that silence and intelligence, the soul of Christ blazed with the flame of God's glory, the radiance of eternity, His own Love, praise, and adoration of God.

He looked into the depths of the Trinity, of which His own Person was, so to speak, the center, and his Sacred Heart, Man's Heart, Human Will, Man's Soul, shone like the sun and overflowed with the fire of an adoration intense, perfect, calm and supreme. It was the adequate, total, integral adoration which alone could give God the glory that really belongs to Him. The flame of that act bursts forth from the depths of the Divine Being of the Man

Christ and speaks God's praise into the very essence of God without tremor and without dismay.

"*Ecce venio* . . . Behold I come to do Thy will, O Lord!" . . .

That act has never ceased. It goes on forever. We have often seen
it without understanding, as it is repeated over and over before
our eyes on our Altars. That act of Love, of Infinite Adoration
would have been the center and source of all spiritual life in time
and in eternity, even if Adam had never sinned and there had been
no captives to redeem . . .

But since there was sin in the world, without an added effort,
almost without an added expense of thought or consideration,
that perfect flame also embraced a cross and consumed all sin. The
God that had come to live among us as Man would also live among
us as Redeemer and: here is the difference. There was one thing
that made the flame of His love burn, if possible, with a more
tremendous intensity: it was the joy that He could even sacrifice
and seem to destroy Himself for the glory of His Father!

✠   ✠   ✠

You are looking for the meaning of Christmas? You cannot help
seeing it, first of all, from the point of view of our own human
misery. But if you want to *celebrate* Christmas, enter into the celebration which is in the soul of the Man-God, Christ!

Where will you find that celebration? Not in noise, but in silence.
Not in restlessness, but in peace. Not in selfishness, but in selfless-
ness. Not in your own misery, but in the greatness and goodness
of God. Not outside your own soul, but within your own soul, and
as deep within it as the point where the spirit, in the invisible,
supra-sensible clarity of grace and faith, makes vital contact with
the Word Who is Christ.

Enter into His peace, His silence, that you may taste His glory,
and realize something of what it means that there has been a
Christmas in our dark world: and realize that there is a feast which
is celebrated at the very roots of all existence!

Is Mysticism Normal?

An interval of almost two years separates Merton's Christmas 1947 meditation from his next original article to appear in *The Commonweal* (November 4, 1949, 94–98), due not only to his work during this period on his volume of meditations, *Seeds of Contemplation*, and his history of the Cistercian Order, *The Waters of Siloe* (published on March 2 and September 5, 1949, respectively), but to his writing for other periodical publications as well. Merton was not absent from *The Commonweal* in the meantime, publishing two reviews, two poems, and two excerpts from unpublished portions of *The Seven Storey Mountain* during the course of 1948. "Is Mysticism Normal?" is closest in focus and tone to the booklet *What Is Contemplation?* first published in December of the previous year (Holy Cross, IN: Saint Mary's College, 1948), and particularly to the revised edition published in England by Burns, Oates & Washbourne in 1950 and in the United States the following year by Templegate.

Merton's answer to the question in his title is, not surprisingly, affirmative, but it is carefully qualified to prevent misunderstanding. Following the Dominican theologian Reginald Garrigou-Lagrange and the Jesuit Joseph Maréchal, he rejects the notion that there are two distinct paths to sanctity, an ordinary way of practicing the virtues and avoiding sins and an extraordinary way of mystical union. At the same time, he emphasizes both that infused contemplation is a supernatural gift of God that cannot be attained by human effort and that many quite holy people have apparently never received this gift. But if infused contemplation is a foretaste of the ultimate union with God in love to be experienced

47

in the beatific vision, he says, it is part of a trajectory that marks the spiritual journey common to every Christian. It is intrinsically related to the charity that is the essence of genuine Christian perfection: "the mystical life is something that is arrived at according to the ordinary laws of normal spiritual development. . . . Therefore there is a *general, remote* call to the mystical life offered to every Christian in the state of grace." All the redeemed are drawn by grace and the gifts of the Holy Spirit into the path of the mystical life, therefore, but it does not necessarily follow, Merton maintains, that all are given the graces of infused, passive mystical prayer, which may be rare but is not thereby to be considered abnormal or discontinuous with more active expressions of the power of the Spirit in people's lives. In fact, the preliminary stages of mystical prayer may often be experienced by "so many *saintly* souls in the active life" who are not consciously aware that their apparently dry and unremarkable prayer actually involves a degree of passive openness and response to the divine presence that differs in degree but not in kind from the higher reaches of mystical union. These are the "masked contemplatives," a term used by Jacques Maritain in his essay "Action and Contemplation" to describe these unconscious mystics (see Merton's February 10, 1949, letter to Maritain [*Courage for Truth*, 24], and *Introduction to Christian Mysticism*, 250–51, n. 694, for the relevant passage from Maritain's essay). Merton adopts this usage here and in the second edition of *What Is Contemplation?* (and will retain it in its extensive revision, *The Inner Experience*, 64) to clarify the meaning of "quasi-contemplatives" found in the original version.

> *The life of grace is not merely natural, it is supernatural.*
> *For a Christian the supernatural itself is the "normal."*

What is the normal fullness of Christian sanctity? What is the spiritual ideal which we should all ordinarily seek, by making use of the graces won for us by Christ on the Cross and dispensed to us through the usual channels? Are there two kinds of Christian sanctity, one reached by an "ordinary" way of everyday virtue, another reached by an "extraordinary" way of mystical graces? Is mysticism designed by God to be the portion of a few extraordinary souls, or does it enter into the normal economy He has planned for us all?

If mysticism is for all, does that necessarily mean that the Christian saint will experience manifest graces of mystical *prayer* also? Or does Christian perfection only imply a dominance of the Gifts of the Holy Ghost, which activate us in the heroic practice of the mystical *life*, without necessarily giving us a recognizably experiential knowledge of the presence and action of God in our souls— which would be classified as infused contemplation or mystical *prayer*? Is there a general call to the mystical *life*, or is the mystical life a special vocation? Is mystical *prayer* a special vocation, or is it even an extraordinary vocation?

These questions have been discussed repeatedly since the first World War. With the passage of time and with the careful study of the French Thomist, Father Garrigou-Lagrange, O.P., who is the chief exponent of the thesis that the mystical life is in the normal way of Christian perfection, it seems that this thesis is being accepted as the more common opinion. Father Maréchal says that "this doctrine echoes the most authentic tradition and now meets with scarcely any opposition."

Yet some people remain in doubt. For one thing, there seem to be very few mystics among us, and, at least so it appears, most of the people in our convents and monasteries and in the world at large seem to have no chance of entering the mystical life. Still, although sanctity, too, is sadly rare, one does meet with men and women who practice real virtue but who, nevertheless, do not appear to have received any mystical graces. Another strong objection to the thesis, and a practical one too, is this: all too often you find Christians who, in a burst of misguided fervor, decide that they are called to mystical prayer and proceed to plunge into an interior life which is a strange concoction of home-made spiritual excitements, cooked up by an overheated imagination. This lasts for a month or two, or even a couple of years, only to end in a nervous breakdown or a relapse into complete moral apathy, tepidity and indifference to the spiritual life.

✠   ✠   ✠

Before answering the question, Is Mysticism Normal? we shall dispose of some preliminary matters. First, no theologian worthy of attention holds that infused contemplation is the essence of Christian perfection, which consists in the union of the soul with God by perfect charity. Charity is of the very essence of perfection. To be a saint is to be perfect in love. Charity, in the saint, unites all the other virtues with itself and in some sense includes them all, and charity unites man with God as with his last end, so that the saint loves God for Himself alone and lives for God alone, excluding all inordinate attachment to anything less than God. Such is the teaching of Saint Thomas on Christian sanctity.

Anyone with experience in the struggle for Christian perfection realizes that there are very virtuous men and women who reach a high degree of perfection without ever receiving the grace of mystical or infused contemplation, at least in a clearly recognizable form, on earth. Such souls may actually reach a higher degree of sanctity than other less perfect souls who, nevertheless do receive the gift of passive, contemplative prayer and an experiential knowledge of God dwelling and acting in their souls. In fact, the grace of infused prayer, far from being perfection, is only another—and very effective—*means* to perfection. It ought to be well known that God often sees fit to grant this grace to Christians who are far from perfection, in order to lead them more rapidly in the ways of virtue and sanctity.

In this respect the doctrine of the Church is that mystical contemplation and the graces of the mystical life are free gifts of God. Although they may be merited *de congruo*, by disposing oneself properly, God may still withhold the enjoyment of these gifts on earth; He gives them to some souls and refuses them to others without our being able to determine exactly why He so dispenses His gifts. All we can do is acknowledge with St. Paul that "each one has his proper gift from God" and that the Holy Spirit distributes these graces according to the function each soul has in the Mystical Body of Christ.

It should not be necessary to add that infused contemplation does not mean visions, ecstasies, revelations or the gift of prophecy. These so-called charismatic gifts are clearly outside the ordinary way of Christian perfection, for they do not belong to the normal means by which God has willed to bring men to union with Himself. They are extraordinary gifts given to individuals not essentially for their own sanctification, but for some special purpose in the spreading of Christ's Kingdom.

Infused contemplation is intimately connected with charity and is an experiential perception of God, as He is in Himself, realized by a union of love with Him, rather than through the medium of images and species which cannot truly represent Him. Jesus Christ, in the Gospels, clearly indicated that to those who loved Him and His Father, and did the will of His Father, there would be granted an intimate and experiential knowledge of God as He is in Himself—that is, of the Blessed Trinity, and this knowledge would be denied to those who did not love Him and who belonged to "the world." "He that loveth me shall be loved of my Father: *and I will love him and manifest myself to him. . . . My Father will love him and we will come to him and make our abode with him*" (John 14:21, 23). "Now we have received not the spirit of this world but the Spirit that is of God, that we may know the things that are given us from God. . . . But the sensual man perceiveth not these things that are of the Spirit of God, for it is foolishness to him" (I. Cor. 2:12, 14).

We are not here claiming that these texts necessarily refer to infused contemplation in the strict sense, although St. Thomas seems to interpret them in that light. They might also refer to a lofty form of acquired contemplation. This is another much discussed point. The highest degree of "acquired" contemplation rejoins and seems indistinguishable from what many writers call "infused."

There is no supernatural contemplation that does not include a generous activity by the Holy Spirit in the soul. The difference between acquired and infused contemplation is not the difference between a contemplation that is entirely active on one hand and one that is entirely passive on the other: it is rather a distinction between a contemplation in which our activity predominates and one in which the activity of the Holy Ghost predominates; in the higher degrees of "passive" contemplation the activity of our own soul is submerged, absorbed by that of the Holy Spirit. Even in acquired contemplation there is an element of passive subjection to the Holy Ghost; otherwise it is not really supernatural contemplation.

✠   ✠   ✠

Now that these preliminaries have been treated, we may examine the main question. What does it mean to say that mysticism is a normal development of the Christian life?

In the first place, every Christian is potentially a contemplative and the end for which we were created is the vision of God and the perfect love flowing from that vision. "This is eternal life, that they may know Thee, the one true God, and Jesus Christ whom Thou hast sent" (John 17:3). The very nature of the human soul, according to the teaching of St. Thomas, points to this end as the highest fulfillment of every capacity implanted in us by our Creator.

There is no doubt, then, that the beatific vision enjoyed by the blessed in heaven, which is the most perfect and super-abundant kind of mystical contemplation, is the normal end of the Christian life. It is what we were made for, it is what Jesus Christ died on the Cross to obtain for us. In this sense, the souls of the saints in heaven are the only truly and completely *normal* Christians and they are the greatest mystics, the most perfect contemplatives. We, on earth, are not leading the life that was planned for us as "normal" by God. Nor are the souls in Purgatory leading the "normal" Christian life. Needless to say, nothing is more *ab*normal than damnation, which leaves the soul, by its own free choice, completely and eternally wrenched out of the place originally planned for man by God.

Nothing is more "normal" than the beatific vision which, nevertheless, completely transcends all our natural powers and is most "extraordinary" if it be compared with our natural way of knowing things; for there God, instead of appearing to us through the medium of abstract or even infused species, becomes Himself as it were the "species" by which we know Him in a direct intuition which is the product of an immediate contact of our intellect with His divine Being! Therefore it is clear that we are not using the word "normal" to mean anything like "natural." The Christian life is not merely natural, it is supernatural, and consequently it is what is *supernatural* that is *normal* in the Christian life.

To say that the mystical life is the normal way of Christian perfection generally means that the mystical life (whether it is actually reached by many or by few does not matter) is, *in itself*, and in the abstract, part of the ordinary system of graces and other means offered by God for the sanctification of men. This means that the mystical life is something that is arrived at according to the ordinary laws of normal spiritual development. Father Garrigou-Lagrange takes the word normal, in this sense, to mean that therefore there is a *general, remote* call to the mystical life offered to every Christian in the state of grace. The mere fact that you are a Christian and are in a state of grace should mean, according to this theory, that by corresponding to grace you may quite normally enter the mystical *life*. Note that we say mystical life and not mystical prayer, for there is a distinction. This will be treated later.

But now, suppose for a moment that the call to the mystical life, instead of being general and offered to all Christians, were a *special* vocation. We do not hold that it is, but even supposing it were, would it therefore be abnormal and extraordinary? Why should it be? The vocation to the priesthood is a *special* vocation: but is it abnormal? Is it extraordinary? The priesthood falls within the normal economy of graces by which God has willed the sanctification of men. He does not will *all* men to be sanctified in the priesthood, but He has willed that some should become saints by faithfully and zealously carrying out the duties of the priesthood. The vocation to the religious life is a *special* vocation. Is it abnormal or extraordinary for a Christian to be sanctified in the cloister? There are many other special vocations that all fall within the limits of the normal Christian life. Even if the vocation to the mystical life, or the vocation to mystical prayer, were to be considered special vocations, it would not necessarily follow that they were *extraordinary* vocations.

This is a distinction that is not generally taken into account. People have often discussed this problem as if there were no alternative between the general call offered to all Christians and a completely extraordinary and esoteric vocation offered to a few stigmatics and prophets.

✠   ✠   ✠

This brings us to the distinction between the *mystical life* and *mystical prayer*, which was mentioned earlier in this article. This particular point was taken up by the too little known Trappist authority on prayer, Dom Vital Lehodey, and it has recently been espoused in this country by my distinguished confrere, Fr. M. Raymond, O.C.S.O. The distinction is essential for a true understanding of the whole question.

The distinction between the *mystical life* and *mystical prayer* is based on St. Thomas's teaching on the Gifts of the Holy Ghost. Indeed, it is upon this Thomist theory of the Gifts that the whole structure of the argument for the normality of the mystical life rests.

Here is the theory, distilled from the masterly treatise of the Spanish Dominican, John of St. Thomas.

We are led to sanctity by the Holy Spirit through what is technically called the "grace of the virtues and of the gifts." This is the normal equipment given us by God to bring us to perfection—that is, to union of love with Him. The Holy Ghost, by grace, illuminates our intellect and inspires and strengthens our will to produce supernatural acts. These acts are produced on two levels. First, according to a "human mode"—that is, through the infused virtues. Here the Holy Spirit moves us to act according to the standards and the regulation of *reason*. Grace enlightens and strengthens our minds and wills to produce acts in which our faculties *move themselves*. And our faculties move themselves according to their own proper and human mode. That is to say, enlightened by grace the reason deliberates, basing its arguments on the principles of the Christian faith, and offers persuasion to the will which then goes into action, perhaps not without a great struggle, and accomplishes a good work which is willed by God.

The second way in which the Holy Ghost moves us to act supernaturally is something altogether higher than this. Here we are enlightened and strengthened, inspired and moved, not according to the human mode but in a way more appropriate to God Himself. Our action is no longer regulated merely by reason and based on deliberation: it accords with a higher standard, the standard of God Himself, which is beyond the grasp of our reasoning. Here the mind does not regulate or adjust itself, but is immediately regulated and adjusted by the Holy Spirit. The will does not get itself together and move itself into action, it *is moved*, passively, by the Holy Spirit. This passivity, however, does not rob us of freedom. On the contrary, our freedom is in a certain sense increased by the action of the Holy Spirit, for "where the Spirit of the Lord is, there is liberty" (II. Cor. 3:17). The immediate presence of the Holy Spirit moving the will makes us slide into action not with labor and difficulty but with a breathtaking ease and suavity and joy which betokens at least a momentary liberation from the "law" of self-love in our members which so frequently and so disastrously conflicts with the law of God. Here, then, instead of moving ourselves by our own power, we move and are moved (there are still *two* cooperating agents!) by the power of the Holy Spirit. The special motion of the Holy Spirit is both the efficient and formal cause of this supernatural activity, and its product is what goes by the name of *heroic virtue*.

The term *mystical life*, as used by the Thomists, applies to this latter mode of activation, where the soul is under the domination of the Gifts of the Holy Ghost. This is what is held to be the normal way of Christian perfection and this mode of supernatural activity belongs to the integrity of Christian saintliness.

✠   ✠   ✠

Mystical prayer is simply a subdivision of the mystical life. Of the seven gifts of the Holy Ghost, some are ordered to the works of the active life, like Fear, Piety, Fortitude. Others are ordered to the works of the contemplative life, to contemplative prayer. Wisdom and Understanding are the Gifts by which the Holy Spirit produces in the soul that immediate experience of God, known and "savored" in a fruitive, though obscure, contact of love which is the hallmark of mystical contemplation.

But one thing must be made clear about the works and activities of the mystical life. The actions which souls under the immediate guidance of the Holy Ghost produce, according to the manner we have described, *need not be essentially extraordinary*. Generally speaking, souls leading the mystical life under the dominance of the Holy Spirit, overcome the usual difficulties of Christian life, but do so with an exceptional perfection and simplicity and modesty and regulation and interior purity which proceed from the direct action of the Holy Spirit and which give their works tremendous merit in the sight of God, although they may be completely ignored by men.

The Thomist thesis is, then, that the *mystical life*, quite apart from manifest graces of mystical prayer, is the normal way of perfection, the ordinary way to sanctity. Among the many proofs, I need only mention one that is exceptionally strong. It is this. Benedict XIV, in a classical statement of the signs of heroic virtue required by the Church before she will beatify a candidate for the honors of the altar, lists them as follows: first, the matter of the acts must be above the common strength of men; secondly, the acts must be performed with great promptitude and ease; thirdly, they must be accomplished with a certain supernatural joy, and finally this must be verified not once but on frequent occasions. These four conditions cannot be verified without the special motion of the Holy Ghost which places a man in what we have called the *mystical life*. From this, it would clearly follow that if the Thomist theory of the Gifts is correct, the mystical life is not only in the normal way of perfection but is required by the Church for beatification.

The question of *mystical prayer* is not so clear. Mystical prayer is a subdivision of the mystical life, and the mystical life is normal.

Therefore mystical prayer is also normal. But a general vocation to the mystical life does not necessarily imply a general vocation to mystical prayer.

In actual fact, the greatest saints are those who combine in themselves all the Gifts of the Holy Ghost in an unusual degree: they excel at the same time in action and contemplation.

But does the perfection of transforming union become the matter of a general call offered to all Christians? From the teaching of the greatest doctors on this subject—for instance, St. Bonaventure, St. Bernard, St. Thomas, and above all St. John of the Cross, it might seem so. St. John of the Cross is so explicit on the point that there can be no room for doubt as to his opinion. He identifies perfect charity with the mystical marriage, as did St. Bernard and the Cistercian theologians of the twelfth century. He even asserts that it is only when one has reached transforming union that one is able to fulfill, completely and in all perfection, the will of God as it [is] laid down for us in the first commandment, because it is only when we have passed through the Dark Night of total mystical purification from every creature attachment and every imperfection, that we are able really to love God with our "whole heart and our whole mind and our whole strength" in all the literal truth of those words.

However, St. John of the Cross himself admits that this perfection is a pure gift which depends entirely on the good pleasure of God, and all theologians agree that no matter if mystical marriage be the *normal term* of the ascent to Christian perfection on earth, great numbers of souls will never in fact reach it, through no fault of their own. Therefore it becomes, in fact, a special vocation.

✠　　✠　　✠

But the most practical angle of the question of mystical prayer is on a much lower level. What Christians need to realize is not so much that the highest level of mystical union is abstractly open to all, but that the lowest level of mystical prayer is really much more common than people imagine.

By this lowest level of mystical prayer, I refer to a prayer which, though infused, at least according to the Thomist sense of the word, is not perceived or realized. It is that latent or "masked" contemplation which would seem to be offered to those who are barred, by temperament or vocation or other circumstances, from ever becoming fully mature contemplatives, and there are many such. Perhaps the majority of Christians will never in fact enjoy the graces of manifest infused contemplation on earth. But it would seem likely that no one who arrives at the degree of perfection in what we have described as the mystical life, will be deprived of the comfort and strength of this masked or latent contemplation. This is the grace given to so many *saintly* souls in the active life who, though their prayer is apparently very humdrum and prosaic, nevertheless find God in an obscure and subtle way in all the activities they perform in His service. There is an unaccountable strength and peace, a certain interior "lift" which takes hold on souls who know how to find God in His will, and which carries them through difficulties and through problems in a way that bears witness to God's intimate presence with them and in them as they go about their duties for His love. They never realize, perhaps, how close He is to them. They know they are not pure contemplatives, and sometimes their relations with God in formal prayer are distressingly commonplace and dull, so that they are perhaps tempted to give up all hope of sanctity, falsely believing that to be saints they have to burn with a flame that they can really feel. And yet, God is with them in their work. They have a wonderful gift, which they themselves can barely appreciate, of finding Him in their daily tasks, in their common round, and in the people they deal with. It is something so diffuse and tenuous that they can never grasp it or explain it, and it does not help them much to try. If they rationalize the experience, they instantly lose hold on their tenuous possession of God and He slips out of their ken.

These are the "masked" contemplatives. They are mystics, but they do not know it. And generally, even if you tell them so, they will not be inclined to believe you. They will always fear that you are joking, and that a term so exalted as that could not possibly apply to them.

The truth is, they are the little ones who will perhaps turn out to be much higher, in heaven, than many who seemed great by more manifest graces of prayer.

✠   ✠   ✠

What, then, is our conclusion?

The mystical life is essentially the normal way of Christian perfection. The mystical life is one to which all Christians, in general, receive a remote call. On the other hand, manifest mystical *prayer*, infused contemplation in the strict sense of the word, may perhaps be listed, though normal, as a *special* vocation. It is not for all in the same sense as the mystical life is for all. However, the mystical life, by its very nature, includes at least a latent element of infused prayer, and the call to the mystical life implies a call at least to masked contemplation.

Self-Denial and the Christian

On February 13, 1950, Merton wrote to his agent, Naomi Burton,
"You wanted me to send all articles through you. Here is one I
promised *Commonweal* for Lent. Edward Skillin is the editor.
I suppose they are in a rush" (*Witness to Freedom*, 126). This final
Commonweal article until the revised "Poetry and Contemplation"
essay appeared in October 1958 was published in the March 31,
1950, issue, dated two days before Palm Sunday of that year
(649–53). Appropriate to the season, it focuses on the ascetic
rather than the mystical life. While it operates in the context of
the traditional distinction between the order of nature and the
order of grace, its focus is on the purpose of self-denial to liberate
the Christian from the power of illusion and to bring about an
authentic self-realization through dying with Christ to sin and
selfishness and thus dying to death itself. Genuine Christian
asceticism, Merton emphasizes, is marked by balance and a sense
of proportion; it is not a rejection of the created world but of a
distorted relationship to material things that expects of them
what they are unable to offer, true satisfaction and the fulfillment
of the most fundamental desires of the human heart, which can
only be realized by the love of God, by a participation in God's
own love for all that God has made, and by the summoning of
all creation to join in the praise and worship of the Creator.
Thus asceticism must be recognized as fundamentally paschal
and intrinsically sacramental and liturgical, as is evidenced in
texts from the prayers of the Mass as well as from the Scriptures
themselves. A merely negative asceticism, a rejection and denigration of the body and of the material world, is a perversion of
both nature and grace. But a lack of mortification, in the root

sense of dying to self—to the false self created not by God but by one's own attachments and disordered appetites—blocks the process of transformation into the image of the risen Christ that is the true goal of authentic spiritual development. Merton's aim here, then, is to rescue the true Christian teaching on self-denial both from its critics and from those ostensible proponents who in fact undermine its true meaning. This article was the only one from this period that eventually found its way into one of the volumes of Merton's essays: it was included in revised form, under the slightly altered title "Christian Self-Denial," in *Seasons of Celebration*, the collection of pieces on the liturgical year published fifteen years later (125–43). Merton considerably augmented and updated the newer version, appearing in the year that concluded the Second Vatican Council, using language that is both more biblical (for example, Merton substitutes *metanoia* for *abnegation*) and more attuned to the spirit of liturgical renewal ("active and intelligent participation" replaces "reading and understanding the prayers of the Mass, and incorporating them into our lives") (see Appendix 1 for a complete listing of all alterations).

Thus the tone of the reworked article does not clash with that of other essays in the volume that had been written more recently. The major point remains basically the same—that authentic Christian self-denial must "lead us to a positive increase of spiritual energy and life"—but whereas the original "keeps encouraging us with the hope of the happiness that lies ahead" and "puts heaven, so to speak, in our hearts here and now," in its revised form the focus shifts more decisively to the present life, as self-denial "keeps encouraging us to understand that our existence in 'the world' and in time becomes fruitful and meaningful in proportion as we are able to assume spiritual and Christian responsibility for our life, our work, and even for the world we live in" and "enables us to enter into the confusion of the world bearing something of the light of Truth in our hearts, and capable of exercising something of the mysterious, transforming power of the Cross, of love and of sacrifice" (*Seasons of Celebration*, 132). These alterations (included in Appendix 1) provide in miniature an illustration of the same process of re-visioning by which *Seeds of Contemplation* (1949) became *New Seeds of Contemplation* more than a decade later (1961).

A life without asceticism is a life of
illusion, unreality, and unhappiness.

Jesus Christ, Who demanded that His disciples leave all things, take up their cross and follow Him, insisted that He was not of this world (John 8:23). The reason is clear. The "world," in this New Testament sense, refers to the society of those who would not and could not know the Living God because they lived according to principles that made the development of the life of grace impossible in their souls. "For all that is in the world is concupiscence of the flesh and the concupiscence of the eyes and the pride of life which is not of the Father but is of this world" (I John 2:16). Jesus told His disciples that even the professionally pious, the Pharisees, whose lives were rigid and externally austere, had made themselves incapable of receiving into their souls the Mission of the Holy Spirit because they "judged according to the flesh" (John 8:15) and He added "it is the Spirit that quickeneth. The flesh profiteth nothing" (John 6:64).

Now this Spirit of God is called by Jesus "the Spirit of Truth, which the world cannot receive because it seeth him not nor knoweth him" (John 14:27). On the other hand, those who are quickened to a divine life in Christ, by this same Spirit, enter into intimate communion with the Truth. They possess the Truth. Truth lives in their souls. And the "Truth has made them free." Christ Himself is the Truth. And to achieve this union with Him, this freedom based on true values and firm adhesion to God's will, we must necessarily purge out of our hearts all attachment to the false values of the world, and all reliance on our own will. For there is no freedom in selfishness, only captivity. And there is no saving vision in the unaided intellect of fallen man. The limited truths he can still perceive seem to serve only to blind him, since in practice he never turns them to the one thing that matters, the glory of God.

Every page of the New Testament forces us to accept the conclusion which St. Paul expressed in such unequivocal language: "We are debtors not to the flesh, to live according to the flesh, for if you live according to the flesh you shall die, but if by the Spirit you mortify the deeds of the flesh, you shall live" (Romans 8:12-13).

There are still too many people who think that Christian abnegation means giving up all the best things in life in order to pay off a grudging debt to a severe Judge in Heaven, Who has a claim on us because we have sinned, and Who means to exact punishment by depriving us of a happiness to which we would otherwise be fully entitled. It is rather a crude error. Yet even those who say they believe in a God of love are capable of making the same mistake, in a subtler and more roundabout way. God, they know, is a God of love. He wants us to be happy. But (and here is where the mistake comes in) they argue that therefore He cannot really want us to deny ourselves after all. You see, they, too, think that our happiness consists in the good things of the present life. They too, perhaps unconsciously, tend to base many of their practical decisions on what St. Paul calls the "wisdom of the flesh."

✠   ✠   ✠

From the few lines of Scripture we have quoted, and from the text in which they are embedded, it is easy to see that far from making us unhappy, Christian self-denial is supposed to help us find perfect happiness by leading us rapidly to the fulfillment of our supernatural destiny. The principles on which St. John of the Cross bases his doctrine in the *Ascent of Mount Carmel* are doubtless rather strong meat and we do not suggest that, in practice, they should form part of the diet of those for whom milk would still be of greater profit. Nevertheless, those principles remain both clear and true. When the great Carmelite says: "In order to arrive at having pleasure in everything, desire to have pleasure in nothing," he is teaching us the quickest way to happiness. The second half of his sentence is so bluntly stated that it may perhaps shock us into forgetting the first. But it is nevertheless true that the passions and desires of fallen human nature, because of their tendency to blind and weaken and exhaust the soul, constantly prevent us from fulfilling our highest capacities and therefore frustrate the need for happiness which is implanted in us all. It has been the constant and uninterrupted teaching of the Fathers and Doctors of the Church since the very first days of Christianity that a life without asceticism is a life of illusion, unreality, and unhappiness.

☩   ☩   ☩

St. Thomas teaches us, in a terrific sentence, the distance between the order of nature and the order of grace. He says that the value of grace in the soul of one just man is greater than the natural value of the entire universe. It is obvious, therefore, that if we are to realize our destinies, to make ourselves what we are intended to be, and find happiness both in this life and in the next, our chief concern should be to develop the life of grace in our souls. In order to do so we have to check and control all those impulses of that other "law in our members" which, as a matter of unpleasant practical fact, conflicts with the life of grace. "The wisdom of the flesh is an enemy to God: for it is not subject to the law of God, neither can it be" (Romans 8:7).

However, no one can really embrace the Christian program of asceticism mapped out in the New Testament, unless he has some idea of the positive, constructive function of self-denial. The Holy Spirit never asks us to renounce anything without offering us something much higher and much more perfect in return. Self-chastisement for its own sake has no place in Christianity. The function of self-denial is to lead us to a positive increase of spiritual energy and life. The Christian dies, not merely in order to die but in order to live. And when he takes up his cross to follow Christ, the Christian realizes, or at least believes, that he is not going to die to anything but death. The Cross is the sign of Christ's victory over death. The Cross is the sign of life. It is the source of all our power. It is the trellis upon which grows the Mystical Vine whose life is infinite joy and whose branches we are. If we want to share the life of that Vine we must grow on the same trellis and must suffer the same pruning. Even healthy shoots of natural life and energy, fruitful branches of our humanity, will have to be cut away. It is not only the evil that is in us that must be renounced. We are even asked to give up many good things: but only in order to get something better. "I am the true vine and my Father is the husbandman . . . every branch that beareth fruit, he will purge it, *that it may bring forth more fruit*" (John 15:1-2). It would scarcely be reasonable to suppose that the vintner attacks the vine with his clippers because he has a grudge against it, and wants to deprive it of its due.

There is no better or more complete manual of ascetical theology than the Missal. Quite apart from the teaching in the Epistles and Gospels, which are the actual word of God, the Church offers us in her collects and other prayers a most exhaustive and monumental theology of self-denial and supernatural living. To *live* the Mass that we all offer, by reading and understanding the prayers of the Mass, and incorporating them into our lives, is the best way to acquire the true Christian sense of abnegation.

☩   ☩   ☩

Christian asceticism is remarkable above all for its balance, its sense of proportion. It does not overstress the negative side of the ascetic life, nor does it tend to flatter human nature by diminishing responsibilities or watering down the truth. It shows us clearly that while we can do nothing without grace, we must nevertheless co-operate with grace. It warns us that we must make an uncompromising break with the world and all that it stands for, but it keeps encouraging us with the hope of the happiness that lies ahead. But what is above all characteristic of the asceticism of the Missal is that it puts heaven, so to speak, in our hearts here and now.

What is the Mass? It is a participation in the death of Christ (by which all our sins are expiated) and in His glorious Resurrection (by which His divine life is made our own) and in His Ascension (by which we enter with Him into heaven and sit at the right hand of the Father). We who offer the Holy Sacrifice and who receive into our hearts the Body and Blood of the Savior are already beginning our heaven here on earth. It is still a heaven possessed only in the darkness of faith and hope: yet the love by which Jesus

unites us to Himself gives us a profound and sweet and experiential certitude of the union of our lives with His life and with one
another in Him. We are already citizens of that Jerusalem that
needs no sun and no moon because Christ is the lamp thereof.
Here, for instance, is what a postcommunion, chosen at random
in the Missal, tells us about the divine life we are already leading
on earth. The Church addresses the Blessed Trinity in these words,
after the priest has received and distributed Communion. "Lord,
may the action of this heavenly gift possess our minds and bodies
so that our natural way of doing things may no longer prevail in
us, but that the effects of this Communion may always dominate
our lives" (15th Sunday after Pentecost).

Here we can see, first of all, that the Church clearly recognizes
what her task is. God has placed in her hands divine instruments
for our sanctification—the Sacraments. In fact, it is He Himself
who, through the Church, works in our lives by means of these
Sacraments. What is He doing in our souls? He is gradually taking
over everything that we have and everything that we are, in order
to gain complete possession of our souls and bodies and all our
faculties, elevating them above the natural level and transforming
them into Himself. In other words, He is substituting His life for
our life, His thoughts for our thoughts, His will for our will. This
process of transformation leads to the end for which we were
created—perfect union with God. It is only when we are perfectly
united to Him that we become our true selves. It is only in Him
that we can find true happiness. It is only in Him that we can
finally appreciate the true value of His creation. If he seems to
deprive us of natural goods, we will find them all restored to us
a hundredfold in Him.

Often in the course of the liturgical year the Church complains,
in our behalf, that we are pressed down under the burden of our
own human activity. That seems strange! To be free to do things
in our own way would appear, at first sight, to be a blessing. But
no. As we enter into the ascetic life and advance in the ways of
self-denial, we find that our biggest obstacle and our biggest burden is this old man of the sea, this body of death, this inescapable
self we carry around with us. He is not our real self at all. He is the

caricature of what we ought to be. But he rides us without mercy and, without the all-powerful help of God, we will never be able to shake him off. And he is the one who makes us act according to the "wisdom of the flesh." He is the father of all our worldliness. He is the one who prevents our liberation from "the world," and our transformation in Christ.

✠   ✠   ✠

And so we must remember that our asceticism is not directed against created things as such. Our real enemy is within our own castle. It is only because this enemy surrounds himself with the images and sensations and delights of created things and thus fortifies himself against all efforts of grace to dislodge him, that we must necessarily fight creatures in order to fight him.

When the Church prays, as she frequently does, that God may give us the grace to despise earthly things and desire the things of heaven, she does not mean to imply that creation is evil: but that the inordinate love of created things is evil.

How does the liturgy look at created things? Everybody knows that the Church, realizing that all creation fell with Adam, intends to raise up all creation together with man, in the New Adam, Christ. It was in Christ that all things were made in the first place. "For in him were all things created in heaven and on earth . . . and he is before all and by him all things consist" (Col. 1:16-17). To deliver creation from the power of evil, the Church has only to associate created things in man's worship of the Creator. Thus they begin once more to serve the purpose for which they were created—to lift man up, body and soul, to God. "For every creature of God is good, and nothing is to be rejected that is received with thanksgiving: *for it is sanctified by the word of God and prayer*" (I. Tim. 4:4). Just take a glance at the liturgy of Holy Saturday, at the *Exultet* (where the bees come in for their measure of praise) and at the blessing of the font (where the Church becomes positively enthusiastic about water, calling it a "holy and innocent creature"). All this tells us what respect the Church has for God's creation. But the fact remains that she has no respect whatever either for the "world" or for the "flesh" and least of all for the devil. These three forces produce mental attitudes, ways of looking at things and doing things, which must be absolutely rooted clean out of the Christian soul.

✠   ✠   ✠

There are two extremes to be avoided. On one hand there is the error of those who believe that creation is evil and who therefore seek salvation and sanctity in an exaggerated asceticism that tries to sever the soul entirely from the rest of creation. This is the spiritual disease called "angelism." But on the other hand there is the error of those who act as if divine charity made no practical demands on human conduct: as if grace were merely a quality injected into our natural lives, making them automatically pleasing and meritorious in the sight of God, without any obligation on our part to live on the supernatural level of faith and Christian virtue. This attitude sometimes usurps the name of "humanism." Concerning those who cherish this view, the twelfth-century Cistercian, St. Aelred of Rievaulx, wrote sardonically: "Although they do not say 'Let us eat, drink and be merry, for tomorrow we die!' they say 'Let us eat, drink and be merry for we are full of charity!' "

True sanctity does not consist in trying to live without creatures. It consists in using creatures in order to do the will of God. It consists in using God's creation in such a way that everything we touch and see and use and desire gives new glory to God. To be a saint means to pass through the world gathering fruits for heaven from every tree and reaping God's glory in every field and farm. The saint is one who is in contact with God in every possible way, in every possible direction. He is united to God in the depths of his own soul, and he sees and touches God in everything and everyone around him. Everywhere he goes, the world rings and resounds (though silently) with the deep pure harmonies of God's glory. Everything he touches is a *sanctus* bell and a call to adoration.

✠   ✠   ✠

But God cannot be glorified by anything that violates the order established by His wisdom. This order demands that man's body, and all that his body uses, be in subjection to his soul, and that man's soul be subject to God. Now this order is absolutely impossible, in our present state, without the generous and even severe practice of mortification. This order was turned completely upside down by original sin. The soul that is outside the orbit of God's grace is not normally governed by reason but by passion. The mere possession of grace does not entirely deliver us from this sad state. It only puts in our hands the weapons by which we must win our freedom, helped by the power of God, through the merits of Christ's Cross, in His Holy Spirit. But the merits of Calvary cannot be applied to a soul that does not in some measure enter into the mystery of Christ's Passion and death and Resurrection. "If any man will come after me, let him deny himself and take up his cross and follow me" (Matt. 16:24). "They that are Christ's have crucified their flesh with its vices and concupiscences" (Galatians 5:24).

We cannot use created things for the glory of God unless we are in control of ourselves. We cannot be in control of ourselves if we are under the power of the desires and appetites and passions of the flesh. We cannot give ourselves to God if we do not belong to ourselves. And we do not belong to ourselves if we belong to creatures.

The real function of asceticism is, then, to liberate us from desires that debase and enslave our souls made for union with God in pure love and even in contemplation. The real purpose of self-denial is to turn over the faculties of our soul and body to the Holy Spirit in order that He may work in us the work of transformation which is His masterpiece, and which puts all the rest of creation to shame.

St. Gregory Nazianzen speaks of the Christian soul as an "instrument played by the Holy Spirit." The aim of asceticism is to keep this instrument in tune. Mortification is not simply the progressive deadening of natural vitality. That is too crude a view. It is rather like the tightening of a violin string. We do not just go on twisting and twisting until the string breaks. That would not be sanctity, but insanity. No: what we must do is bring the strings of the delicate instrument, which is our soul, to the exact pitch which the Holy Spirit desires of us, in order that He may produce in us the exquisite melody of divine love that we were created to sing before the face of our heavenly Father. Neglect of this truth would lead to a false, merely quantitative asceticism that would put too much stress on mere spiritual athletics, and do nothing to develop the deep spiritual capacities of the soul.

False asceticism is not in tune with the Holy Ghost because it is a perversion of grace. And it is also a perversion of nature. It does nothing to perfect the soul. It frustrates God's work and diminishes all our natural and supernatural capacities for good. The false ascetic is usually one who develops a kind of split personality. One half of his personality takes up arms against the other half and tries to destroy it. But it does not succeed. What happens then? The suppressed half of this unfortunate being withdraws into the depths of the soul, and there healthy natural tendencies turn into unhealthy and vicious dispositions of soul. That is why those who go about their self-denial in a crude and human way are often proud and irritable and uncharitable. That is why men who might have been saints have become fanatics and have persecuted the saints and burned them at the stake.

☩   ☩   ☩

The function of self-denial is to bring peace to the soul that is troubled by all the cares and worries and sorrows and unrest that follow inevitably from attachment to created things. Asceticism is the arch enemy of all worry because it roots out every plant from which the fruits of anxiety grow. The ascetic, then, will be a tranquil and happy man. His will be a simple and limpid soul, like a pool of clear water into which the sunlight of God's presence can enter without obstacle, to illumine and penetrate all. But this tranquility depends on the virtue of discretion. God demands that all Christians deny themselves but He does not ask the same kind of renunciation from a housewife with ten children to look after as from a Cistercian monk. In the long run, it might well happen that the housewife might turn out to be more mortified than the monk: but she is not expected to do penance in exactly the same way. Her self-denial will be measured by the duties of her state as a wife and as a mother.

Whatever may be the mode and measure of self-denial that God asks of us (and this is a matter that cannot really be decided without prayer and spiritual direction) all Christian asceticism is characterized by wholeness and by balance. Christ admits of no division. He who is not with Jesus is against Him. There is no fellowship between light and darkness, between the temple of God and idols. God asks us to give Him everything. But we have already said what that means: using all creatures for God alone. Consequently our asceticism must always be balanced. The true ascetic is not one who never relaxes, but one who relaxes at the right time and in the right measure, who orders his whole life, under the direct guidance of the Holy Spirit, so that he works when God wants him to work and rests when God wants him to rest and prays constantly through it all by a simple and loving gaze that keeps his heart and mind united with the Blessed Trinity in the depths of his soul.

To such a one the Cross is always a source of strength and peace. "Because I am nailed to the Cross with Christ," says St. Thomas Aquinas, paraphrasing St. Paul and commenting on him, "because I am nailed to the Cross with Christ I have power to do good." Without the Cross, there is little spiritual vitality in our labors for God and His Church.

✠　　✠　　✠

In a world in which there is so much involuntary suffering, it is not strange that there should be many men and women who begin to discover in themselves a totally unfamiliar desire to take upon themselves penances and mortifications for which there is no strict obligation. That is a good sign. Wherever the Spirit of God works, He draws men away from the "wisdom of the flesh." He lets them savor something of the sweetness of God, and this makes them aware of the corruption that is in the world around them. Pleasures and achievements that once delighted their spirit now turn to ashes as soon as they are savored, and it becomes a pleasure for these generous souls to do without the good things that most men have come to consider almost indispensable.

But the more the Holy Spirit draws these souls to God, the more they realize that sanctity is not just a matter of "ascetic practices." Fasts and penances take on their true importance when they are seen as means to an end. That end is the total gift of ourselves to God in an interior abnegation that penetrates to the very depth and substance of the soul, a holocaust that leaves nothing that our pride can still contemplate with satisfaction. Rare are the souls that travel this far. But theirs is a happiness that is sublime. Since they no longer find joy in anything but God, they find supreme joy in everything, because God is all in all.

Part II

Articles from Other Periodicals

Death of a Trappist

Reflecting on requests for articles from various periodicals in a September 7, 1947, journal entry, Merton writes, "last week I had to write one for a new magazine without much of a budget called *Integrity*" (*Entering the Silence*, 105). This was a lay-run magazine committed to the principles of Catholic Action, founded in New York a year earlier, which identified itself on the cover of each issue as "published by lay Catholics and dedicated to the task of discovering the new synthesis of religion and life for our times." Its contributors at one time or another included Dorothy Day, Catherine de Hueck Doherty, Caryll Houselander, Fr. Paul Hanley Furfey, and even Maria von Trapp, as well as Thomas Merton. Not only the authors but also the staff were unpaid during the decade of the magazine's existence, which ended in 1956. This first of Merton's two contributions (*Integrity* 2.2 [1947], 3–8) aims to demythologize the popular conception of Trappists as fixated on death, extending all the way back to Armand de Rancé's reform of the Abbey of La Trappe in seventeenth-century France, which had so fascinated his contemporaries and subsequent generations of commentators inclined to the gloom of a Gothic romanticism. Despite the title of this essay, Merton's focus is on the Order as descending first and foremost from its twelfth-century founders and their healthy contemplative spirit rather than from the later reformers, whose emphasis on penitential practices did not fully embody the original Cistercian charism and vocation. Far from being obsessed by death, Merton claims, Cistercian monks with their balanced life of liturgical and private prayer and manual labor are able to regard death as the culmination of a simple and balanced life marked by awareness of the presence of God. In this context, the rituals and practices that surround the death of a monk take on a dignity and meaning that are seldom experienced in the secular world. Merton's vivid descriptions of the community gathered at the deathbed to witness and assist at the final anointing with their prayer, of the pairs of monks keeping vigil throughout the night in shifts in the abbey church with their dead brother, and of what came to be called the "green burial" of the body, without embalming and without a coffin, convey the stark simplicity of a Cistercian practice far different from the lurid and macabre accounts mentioned earlier in the article. Merton concludes his discussion not in the abbey cemetery but in the presence of God, where a monk who has undergone his purgatory on earth and been purified of all selfishness enters into "an everlastingly perfect mutual giving of the soul to God and of God to the soul." But as he typically does in his articles on monastic topics in this period, Merton finishes by reminding his readers that such an immediate passage into divine life is not reserved for those under religious vows and that the perfection of charity is no less possible for the housewife and the laborer than for the monk, a point of particular relevance to the editors of this new magazine and their intended audience, struggling to make the Gospel visible and effective in the world.

Anyone who wants to know something about the death of a Trappist must first have a reasonably clear idea of how a Trappist lives. Unfortunately, too many have (at the back of their minds) a completely impossible conception of the Trappist monk dwelling in the semi-darkness.

The monk who abides in these uneasy shadows is a lanky ghost of a man, half starved and not a little frantic with too much concentration on the skull he always has before him. His hands are calloused, but not with useful labor, only with digging his own grave. He digs a little bit out of that grave each day, heaving profound sighs and crooning over and over to himself *"Memento mori! Memento mori!* Remember that thou shalt die." As he is by now getting on in years his grave is well over a hundred and fifty feet deep and he wears himself out climbing in and out of the thing on moss-covered ladders. When he finally emerges at the top he fumbles around for his discipline and begins beating himself on the shoulders with it, doubtless in an honest effort to speed the coming of the day when he can stay in the earth for good and all.

It is extremely fortunate that such people never existed. But the mere fact that the legend of their existence is so tenacious is something that makes Trappists insist on being called by their true name. The word "Trappist" is an outmoded nickname for the Cistercian Order of the Strict Observance. It comes from La Trappe, an important monastery of the Order in Normandy, where the famous Abbé De Rancé instituted a reform of the Cistercian Order in the seventeenth century. The Cistercian life is nothing but the Rule of St. Benedict in the strict interpretation that was given to it by the founders of the Abbey of Cîteaux, in France, in the twelfth century. Penance plays a great part in the life, but only as a means to an end. The Cistercian is a contemplative monk, and the fullness of the contemplative vocation is an intimate knowledge of God experienced, as it were, in the darkness of faith and in the contact that is established by a pure and supernatural love. The chief aim of the monk is to empty himself of all the trivial and accidental concerns of worldly existence in order to live for the one thing necessary, *frui Deo*, the perfect love that draws us into such close likeness to God that we are said to be transformed into Him, lost in His infinite perfections as a drop of water is lost in a gallon of wine.

Obviously a lugubrious and monomaniacal insistence on the physical aspects of death to the exclusion of everything else would be fatal to such a vocation, because it would be almost entirely irrelevant.

If Trappists have been accused in the past of creating an almost entirely mortuary ideal of the spiritual life, it is the fault of the romantic and pre-romantic movements in French literature. Poets like Chateaubriand got hold of De Rancé and his Trappists and turned the whole thing into a macabre grand-opera according to the taste of his day. But Chateaubriand is one of the most completely unreliable writers that ever existed. He wrote a novel called "René," part of which is laid in the United States. He shows us, for instance, his hero meditating on the brink of Niagara Falls and listening to the "roaring of the crocodiles" on the rocks below. So don't believe anything Chateaubriand tells you about Trappists.

Last year, Father Anselme Dimier, a Cistercian monk of the Abbey of Tamié in the Alps, brought out an interesting little book called *La Sombre Trappe* to trace all these absurdities to their source.

Once all this has been said, to clear the air, we may consider how a Cistercian monk looks at death, how his life prepares him to meet death.

There is no need for a man to make his drinking cup out of a skull in order to remind himself of the elementary fact that he will not live forever. But, nevertheless, we all need to be reminded of it. It is one thing to admit, intellectually, the obvious truth that the world can never offer us satisfactions that cannot be taken away; but it is quite another thing to live in practice as if temporal things were not ends in themselves and worldly pleasures were not destined to last forever. Scripture reminds us, "In all thy works remember thy last end and thou shalt never sin" (Eccli. vii, 40). The implication is that this is one of the things we most easily forget—otherwise there would not be so much sin.

People who have the misfortune to live outside of monasteries, in a world that seeks only to enrich itself by the exploitation of every appetite that can be forced beyond the limits of order, really need some systematic method of reminding themselves of death. One might think that the spectacle of a society that is in its last agony ought to be a forceful enough reminder. The smell of decay that comes out of every movie-theatre and night club ought to be enough to keep us thinking of the grave. But it takes grace to detect these things and too many people have lost their spiritual sense of smell. . . .

Inside monasteries, above all contemplative monasteries, it is a different matter. Once he is out of the novitiate the Cistercian monk seldom needs to make a systematic meditation on death, although discursive reflection on the "last things" is such a fundamental weapon in the spiritual life that everyone will keep it in reserve against an emergency. But a contemplative who forced himself, with too much of a stubborn insistence, to keep picturing decaying bodies and so forth, would certainly ruin his spiritual life. The aim of all discursive meditations is to convince us of our need of God and of God's power to help us. When these convictions bear fruit, as they soon do, in a permanent affective "thirst" for the presence and contact of God, meditation is absorbed into a fundamentally simple and uniform interior "attitude" which accompanies the monk everywhere. His soul becomes like a sunflower that follows the Divine source of all light and warmth wherever it goes. *Oculi mei semper ad Dominum.* Its eyes find rest only in constant, silent looking towards God. That is the essence of its prayer.

More than by any system of meditations, this "attitude," this permanent spirit of prayer, in which prayer becomes as natural and as easy and as simple as breathing, is nourished by the liturgy and by spiritual reading.

A Cistercian could really afford to dispense with formal meditations on death altogether if he follows the liturgy. The Cistercians recite the Office of the Dead on an average six times a month, and there are four "solemn anniversaries" during the year, when the Office of the Dead and a Pontifical Requiem are sung. The monks know the principal parts of that office by heart, and could sing whole passages of the chant without need of a book. Consequently, it may often happen when one is out at work in the woods and fields that some snatch of chant from one of the responsories of the Office of the Dead may start going in the monk's mind. There is a peculiar pathos in the sober and austere Gregorian melodies of that office, and it brings out all the humility and helplessness that pleads to God in the tremendous words: *Libera me Domine de morte aeterna.* . . .

What is much more fruitful for the soul is a Cistercian funeral. Hardly a year goes by in which someone in the community does not at least receive the Last Sacraments. In fact Cistercians are much more often anointed than buried. The grace of the Sacrament may keep an old Brother going for another year or two. But in any case, the whole community assists at the ceremony, praying and chanting psalms. You learn more about death by coming face to face with it, through liturgical prayer, than you would get out of books and meditations if you plugged at them for a hundred years.

When a Cistercian actually does die, he is taken down to the monastic church in procession, in an open bier, dressed in his religious habit. He is placed in the middle of the choir with a candle and crucifix at his head and a stoup of holy water at his feet, and until he is buried, two monks will always be sitting by the body, day and night, reciting psalms alternately in a low voice. They take turns to perform this office of charity. At night they take long two-hour shifts, so that the constant going and coming may not wake up the others in the common dormitory.

Sometimes these night wakes fall to the lot of a couple of novices, and there is no question that it makes a deep impression. The huge empty church becomes very dark and very silent, and the body in the open bier does not seem to lie as still as it ought to, in the flickering candle light; but you are also very much aware of another presence—where the sanctuary lamp also flickers before the tabernacle—and taking your courage in both hands you start murmuring the Latin words of the psalms. It is strange how quickly the time goes, and when you suddenly realize that your watch is over and that you must return to your straw mattress and bed of planks, you are somehow unwilling to leave. While you were praying there, a deep and sane and vivifying sense of fellowship was growing up that linked you in some mysterious way with the soul to which that body once belonged and to which it will one day be returned. And as you walk through the dark echoing cloister you are no longer afraid of death or of dead bodies but you see them as they are—sad, inevitable things whose sorrow is not without an infinitely merciful remedy.

Praying for the dead in this real and down-to-earth fashion brings you an almost experimental appreciation of the doctrine of the Communion of Saints. One really feels bound in a mysterious and powerful solidarity with these souls, a solidarity that will last forever and which is rich and fruitful in its exchange of graces. The souls of the monks who have died before us come constantly back to our minds and we offer the thought to God in the chalice of some Mass that is being celebrated somewhere in the world at that moment; and in return we feel that many favors have come to us from those who have been grateful for our prayers.

Perhaps the most dramatic thing of all is the way the monk is buried. He is lowered into the ground without a coffin, without a bier. The monastery infirmarian goes down into the grave and covers the face of the corpse and as soon as he climbs out again the earth begins to fall and the dead Cistercian disappears. And yet to many this simplicity and poverty have something about them that is immensely clean in comparison with the nightmare of fake luxury and flowers with which the world tries to disguise the fact of death. It is not the burial of a monk, wrapped in no other shroud than the clothes he always wore, that is frightening; no, it is those embalmed corpses rouged up to look like wax-works and couched in satin cushions that terrify the heart and make even the healthy smell of flowers horrible by the association they contract with undertakers and funerals.

But the most important thing is not how the body of a Cistercian is buried; that is trivial. The real question is: how does such a soul enter into the presence of God?

The death of a true contemplative is inevitably the crown of a life of contemplation. It is the final liberation of a soul from all that impeded it, prevented it from seeing God, held it back from the perfect possession of God and restrained its swift flight to the center towards which it has tended with the almost irresistible gravitation of pure love. At last the body breaks like a web and the soul leaps out, exulting like a flame into the blinding glory of God.

There is no purgatory for the perfect contemplative, because there is nothing left; his liberation is complete. He has had his purgatory on earth, in years of searing, searching interior trials, years of charity and humility and poverty and obscure labor that have stripped him of layer after layer of selfishness and imperfection, and reduced him to nothing in his own eyes. He has been delivered from his own selfishness and his own callousness and hardness of heart by years of sacrifice. The penetrating fire of infused love has made all selfishness intolerable for him, and it has purged him slowly and inexorably of every desire for created pleasure, every ambition, every hope of fame or power; for years all these things have been intolerable to him. The things that cause other men pleasure have caused him nothing but pain, because of the agonizing sense of their insufficiency they brought with them. The things that seem to slake other men's thirst only increase his to a burning torture, and he has long since learned to refuse them all, as Christ refused the vinegar on the Cross. He has long since acquired that wisdom which is best recognized, according to St. Bernard, by the ability to rejoice in suffering because then we truly know we are rejoicing for no selfish motive, but only in the will of God. He has now arrived at that perfection of love which seeks nothing for itself and yet even loves itself perfectly in God, seeing itself as God sees it, loving itself because it holds within itself the perfect reflection of God, cleaned of every stain of selfishness that makes one different from God.

When the last shred of that self-love which constituted a barrier, a difference between the soul and God, has fallen away, the likeness of the soul to its Creator and Exemplar is now perfectly restored; nothing remains but the confirmation and sealing of this union in the glory of an everlasting vision, an everlastingly perfect mutual giving of the soul to God and of God to the soul.

There has never been written anywhere a better description of such a death than that which St. John of the Cross gives us in his *Living Flame of Love.*

> The death of such souls is very sweet and gentle, more so than was their spiritual life all their life long, for they die amid the delectable encounters and sublimest impulses of love. . . . For this reason David said that the death of saints in the fear of God was precious for at such a time all the riches of the soul come to unite together *and the rivers of love of the soul are about to enter the sea, and these are so broad that they seem to be seas already.* (Peers trans. iii, 135)

That is the way the saints, the contemplatives die. Does that mean that such perfection and such a going forth to God is reserved only for those who have lived all their lives in a cloister? Far from it. It may well happen that a Cistercian monk, by failing to make the proper use of the means God has put at his disposal, may be far less perfect than some poor housewife, some laborer in the world. But the secret of that sanctity is the same: the perfection of charity which is most easily and quickly reached by union with God in contemplation. Is this an extraordinary grace that is reserved only for special souls? No! Perfection and the means to perfection are accessible to all, and those who want to travel the road that ends with such an entrance into the glory of heaven have only to set foot on the road by praying to Him Who said ask and you shall receive. They have only to begin leading an interior life and the rest of the way will be made plain.

A Trappist Speaks on People, Priests and Prayer

In a January 4, 1948, journal entry, Merton wrote: "Before Christmas I got a letter from *The Messenger of the Sacred Heart*, of all things, asking for an article on contemplation and the priesthood. Father Anthony told me to refuse. That much thinking I managed to get done for me by somebody else! Yesterday Fr. Lynch came back at me again for an article for his *Messenger*. He said he was trying to turn the magazine upside down and make it intelligent. I don't know what all the old ladies will say when they discover he is trying to rob them of the confectionary they have been getting out of the *Messenger* for the last 100 years! But Fr. Anthony said I could write the article. I would do anything to help clean the mush out of the devotion to the Sacred Heart. It is a job that needs doing almost as badly as anything else in the universe!" (*Entering the Silence*, 155–56). *The Messenger of the Sacred Heart* was the monthly publication of the Apostleship of Prayer, a worldwide church-sponsored organization that chose particular prayer intentions to be remembered each month, as generations of Catholic school graduates will recall. The biographical headnote for Merton's article, which appeared in the April 1948 issue (51–61, 89–90), notes that the author "is known in religion as Fra Louis Merton, O.C.S.O. He is now a Trappist monk at Gethsemane [*sic*], Ky. He also happens to be perhaps the most distinguished Catholic poet in the United States." It is as "A Trappist," if not as a poet, that Merton "Speaks on People, Priests and Prayer" here—the implication apparently being that when a Trappist, popularly thought to be vowed to silence, speaks, he must have something to say worth listening to. As Merton's comments in his journal suggest, the intellectual level of *Messenger* articles was not generally very high, aimed as it was at a broad, not in the main highly educated readership. While the 1948 editor's intent was to elevate the tone and content of the magazine, Merton's contribution is clearly intended to take into account the less sophisticated tastes and uncomplicated piety of the target audience; in it he adopts a somewhat more didactic voice than in other articles of this period, instructing readers at the outset concerning their "special obligation during this month of April to pray for more numerous holy priests," evidently that month's prayer intention. While Merton freely cites both an encyclical of Pope Pius XI and its subject, Saint Thomas Aquinas, he acknowledges that Thomas's description of wisdom "is abstract language, indeed" and after citing the Thomistic term "co-naturality" helpfully adds, "This phrase means that we know what God is like because we ourselves have been made like Him by our perfect love of Him." This sort of patient explaining of rather challenging concepts continues throughout the article, as do the hortatory directives, e.g., "You must pray that Catholic priests always be something far more and far better than the other professional men in their town." It is also noteworthy that he nowhere extends the focus on the call to contemplation that is given to priests to include the laity, as he customarily does in articles for other magazines. The role of the layperson seems to be limited to praying for priests and for the development of their interior life; this is the "good part of the responsibility" for the world's transformation that belongs to lay readers, rather than aspiring to contemplation or for that matter engaging in Catholic Action themselves. One reason for this difference in focus is no doubt that Merton is reinforcing the call of the Apostleship of Prayer to its members to devote their prayer to that month's intention, but another is probably the fact that Merton knows his audience and does not propose that they attempt more than many if not most of them would feel themselves able to or called to carry out.

If it is true that a people will be as good and as great as is its priesthood, it is also true in a very important sense that the greatness of a priesthood will be determined by the people themselves.

That is because, first of all, priests come from the people; and secondly because their virtues depend so much upon the prayers of the people. It is therefore your special obligation during this month of April to pray for more numerous holy priests. These few pages are intended to explain some of the gifts for which you will be praying—and if God is giving and will give more of these things to the Church today, it will be due largely to your response to this Papal summons to prayer.

At the end of this year's June, it will be twenty-five years since Pius XI published one of his greatest Encyclicals: "*Studiorum Ducem.*" It is one of a series of modern Papal documents on St. Thomas Aquinas, and its theme is this: that the Angelic Doctor is a model for priests and for seminarians, not only in his chastity and his science but, above all, in his deep interior life—that exalted union with God which made him one of the Church's great contemplatives.

The heart of "*Studiorum Ducem*" is this: that the chief characteristic of the sanctity of St. Thomas Aquinas is to be found in his preeminent wisdom: and this wisdom is twofold. The Angelic Doctor excelled, says Pius XI, not only in acquired wisdom, but also in that infused wisdom so intimately connected with the humility, the prayer and charity of the great saints. And the Pope quotes from the "*Summa*" St. Thomas' own classical description of this wisdom—which consists, he says, in a right judgment concerning the things of God. That is abstract language, indeed, but the context brings out the difference between acquired wisdom, which knows God through the labor of reasoning, and that other higher wisdom which is a gift of the Holy Ghost. And, says St. Thomas, we come to know God "because of a kind of co-naturality with Him." This phrase means that we know what God is like because we ourselves have been made like Him by our perfect love of Him.

Pius XI would not have held St. Thomas up as a model for priests if it were impossible for the average priest to aspire to the same kind of sanctity, the same kind of interior life. It is understood that God does not destine every priest to be another Aquinas in learning, and it is also quite clear that infused wisdom remains a pure gift of God to which no effort of ours can attain. But once these obvious limitations are recognized, Pius XI is telling priests in that Encyclical: St. Thomas is your model. Imitate him in his love of truth, his zeal for learning, and, above all, aspire to the joys and to the perfection of that altogether supernatural and divine knowledge of Him which the Holy Ghost brings us in the perfection of His gifts. God will not refuse these gifts to those who desire them with a pure intention and who labor to dispose themselves to receive them by growing in love as far as they are able to do so. Finally, according to Pius XI, the ultimate purpose of theology as taught by the Angelic Doctor is to lead us to a life of intimate union with God. The fruit of theology should be a great love of God.

Thus, even when we remember the complaints of the Sacred Heart to St. Margaret Mary about the neglect of His gifts and graces, we are confronted with a consoling truth: Christ came to earth to lead us to the highest perfection of sanctity, to the highest joy, the most perfect participation in His life. The neglect He spoke of may be tragic indeed, but there remains this immensely consoling fact: Christ's love is always there, His mercy is the same from generation to generation; His gifts are always with us if we will dispose ourselves to receive them.

We shall pray, above all because of the terrible needs of our time, for priests who will have a deep and intimate contact with the source of all truth and all happiness, men who should be saturated with the peace which Christ came to bring, who amid duty and routine will not be without a deep interior satisfaction, will not be without the strength and spiritual growth and vivifying union with God that Christ intended for them with such earnest desire.

You must pray that Catholic priests always be something far more and far better than the other professional men in their town. It is not easy for priests to be holy. They have the burden of a busy day, as have the banker and the insurance agent and the real estate man. They have their living to make, their duties to perform, a church or a school to build. They have to run drives and raise money. And they have other chores: they have to sit in the confessional, they have to rack their brains over other people's marriage problems.

A Catholic priest, especially in America, where the Church is growing so rapidly, has a great deal to do. He must be active. But the graces of prayer or contemplation are very often given with a view to the active apostolate. Christ wants His priests to be prayerful not merely for their own strength, their own sanctification and their own satisfaction; above all He wants them to overflow with the fire of His divine wisdom and pour it out upon the world so that all men may wake up and leave their hopeless search for happiness where it cannot be found—in material things!

Two world wars have shaken materialistic culture to the depths of its quaking foundations, and the whole world is full of unquiet men thirsty for peace, hungry for a truth that is objective and solid and lasting. They are sick of the deceptions of the civilization their dumb appetites have built for them. And they already halfconsciously realize that their very dissatisfaction is an argument for the claims of the one religion which has outlasted twenty centuries in real, undisturbed unity and perfect, harmonious continuity, and with such great fruits of holiness in the lives of its great saints and theologians and writers and artists and architects and all the rest.

These men of our times often know and appreciate more of Catholic tradition than we sometimes think, and they instinctively expect to find in any Catholic priest something of what they realize to have been present in men like St. Thomas Aquinas. These men of good will wish to sense in the priest to whom they go to confide their troubles the very opposite of the nervous, active, hectic, restless dissatisfaction which is eating their own hearts out. Let them but come in contact with men who have the beginnings of an interior life, who live by deep faith, who are not afraid to suffer for God, who drink deep draughts from theology and Scripture and incorporate what they read into their lives by meditation—let your good pagan come into contact with such men and the effect is altogether wonderful.

Fortunately, there are thousands of priests like that in the Church. They have kept themselves interiorly free from the world and its business in order to be ready to absorb and receive something that they felt God would some day, somehow begin to tell them about

Himself. They want to keep their lives simple. They are obsessed with an urgent, insistent need to cut out the non-essentials with which a priest's life so easily becomes cluttered. They feel that there is "one thing necessary," and what it is they cannot quite define: but it is a constant, yet peaceful hunger deep in their hearts, a hunger for the peace which Christ alone can give them, a hunger for a light and strength which comes to them when they can be alone in the church with their God, and close their eyes and enter into His wordless peace. And it is for their benefit that God in His Providence has inspired theologians to enter more and more, in our day, into the meaning of the interior life and Christian perfection. And that is why our century is seeing, among other things, a profoundly important revival and simplification of Christian spirituality in its deepest essentials.

But one thing cannot be repeated too often: if those whom God has selected for His special work in the Church are to be able to communicate this interior spirit and peace to a world which is so restless and tortured, it will be largely the fruit of the prayers of the laity. God will surely hear this prayer of mutual charity, of laymen for priests and priests for them.

That Christian perfection of which we have been talking is nothing but perfection in charity; and if wisdom in the sense in which we have used the term is to be an integral part of perfection, it is inseparable from charity and grows with it and flourishes together with it. This was the teaching of St. Bernard of Clairvaux and St. John of the Cross. For both of these great saints, contemplation, the highest wisdom, is nothing else but the pure love of God, and the highest contemplation is simply an aspect of the most perfectly selfless love.

The fire of this wisdom is nothing else than an intensification of charity, and when it burns in the soul of a man it tends by its very nature to consume and eradicate pride and all the other traces left in us by the fall of our First Parents and our own actual sins.

Therefore, the soul who really means to answer the call of God to a deeper interior life will find himself on the Way of the Cross. That does not mean however that the soul must steel itself to bear the extraordinary sufferings which we read in the lives of great saints who had a special vocation to suffer. The Holy Ghost does not intend to treat every man like Jeremias or Job.

Indeed, we do not have to go up to Heaven and bring down the gifts of the Holy Ghost for ourselves. They have already been implanted in us by Baptism, and they are only waiting for us to be generous and uncompromising in all the ordinary duties and events of our lives, that we may progress in virtue to the point where the gifts will be able to "take over" and carry us forward on our way to sanctity. The way to contemplative prayer is a way of simplicity and generosity in the ordinary things of life. Yet someone will say: if that is all, why is it that there are not many more contemplative people in the world than there are? The answer to that is the following essential difference that distinguishes a contemplative soul from the usual active Christian.

The former maintains himself, in all that he does, in a habitual state of inner attention to God. His soul is like the sunflower, always turned toward the Light. He says with David: "*Oculi mei semper ad Dominum* (My eyes are ever on the Lord)." The gaze of his soul is directed with an ever more searching hunger toward the heart of the darkness in which he is immersed, hoping to recover some faint glimpse of the One who sums up in Himself all that the soul is and has and aspires to be. Others will seek a kind of drug in activity and movement and business and preoccupations and affairs. But the truly prayerful man will turn his eyes with greater urgency, in the midst of external works, toward the God who tends to hide Himself when one goes out from His calming presence to do battle among the affairs of men.

And, of course, it will be through such souls that God will produce his most wonderful effects in the world of action and in the social world. If then you wish such a world to live in, a good and a great world, dominated by the spirit of God and of peace, pray that He may always give us such men. Yours is a good part of the responsibility. Therefore pray.

Contemplation in a Rocking Chair

Merton's second contribution to *Integrity* appeared nine months after the first (2, no. 11 [1948]: 15–23), and just four months after his article in *The Messenger of the Sacred Heart*. It makes considerably greater demands on its audience than the latter and takes a much more confrontational stance toward contemporary society than the former. For an article written today, the title "Contemplation in a Rocking Chair" would almost certainly have a positive connotation, suggesting a tranquil openness to the divine presence or perhaps some "aging as sage-ing" reflections on the later stages of the spiritual journey. But Merton's intent here is to undermine any complacent supposition that there is some easy and comfortable shortcut to contemplation that does not require the complete detachment and self-surrender that Jesus demands of his disciples in calling them to take up their cross and follow him. Merton no doubt knew that his fierce attack on bourgeois smugness and self-satisfaction and its identification of scapegoats for one's own failures and inadequacies would find a receptive audience in the subscribers to this new journal of Catholic radicalism, especially those who would be more apt to associate a rejection of middle-class materialism and the pursuit of worldly success with active engagement in the works of mercy than with a commitment to contemplative stillness. Merton's intent is to point out that contemplation is incompatible with the superficial optimism of a worldly ideology but is likewise in danger of being co-opted by it. He warns that the contemporary spirit is all too often ready to settle for appearance rather than substance, for illusion rather than reality, because appearances and illusions do not disturb or challenge the dominant culture's definition of the good life. He also points out that such a perspective can infect one's understanding of contemplation as readily as that of other essential dimensions of authentic human existence. The evasive emptiness of quietism can easily and unconsciously substitute for the authentic self-emptying of surrender to God. A craving for sensible consolation in prayer can become simply another, more subtle, manifestation of the dominant culture's elevation of self-fulfillment as the primary goal of life. Conversely, an apparent rejection of quietistic inertia can easily become the equally evasive cult of activism in which keeping busy is both a way to avoid facing oneself and one's need for transformation and a way to reinforce the erroneous perception characteristic of modern society that what one does determines who one is. As a model for a genuine Christian alternative to the dominant culture and its relentless quest for success as measured by criteria of wealth or pleasure or power, Merton proposes Francis of Assisi, the bourgeois who literally stripped himself, thereby rejecting his privileged status to identify with and to follow the poor Christ. (Of course, even Francis can be and has been domesticated by a reduction of his uncompromising discipleship to an inoffensive, sentimental caricature.) Ultimately Merton calls for a thorough rejection of anything less than the knowledge and love of the true God, which is the true gift of contemplation.

Perhaps one of the most characteristic things about "middle-class culture" is its genius for evasions. One of the fundamental traits of bourgeois society seems to be the complex structure of fictions and abstractions which men have built around themselves as a screen behind which human nature can be as small and as greedy and as mean as it pleases without being ridiculed or disturbed. We have been living, especially for the last two centuries, in a society overcrowded with scapegoats. We excel in surrounding ourselves with straw men on which we shift all our responsibilities. Or, if we happen to be a bit belligerent, we keep them there in order to have a target for our anger when our conscience tempts us to be dissatisfied with our own selves. But behind it all are the souls of individual men and women, each infected with the same disease, each one trying to convince himself that he is not sick by fixing the sickness on some big, monumental abstraction, on something that exists more in the minds of men than in reality.

By a strange irony, this habit has become so deeply ingrained in the minds of men of our day that even the term *bourgeoisie* has assumed a prominent place as one of the middle class's favorite scapegoats. We who have had the misfortune of being born into the middle class try to forget about it, try to dissociate ourselves from it by making fun of it as if we had been born and bred somewhere in interstellar space and then came down to earth to observe the strange activities of other men.

Nevertheless, the truth remains that we who are Catholics and mean to take our religion seriously must, without any doubt or hesitation or compromise, do everything we can to fight our way out of this sticky and unpleasant social matrix in order to recover our true identity in Christ. Remember that for us whose background is the middle class and its materialism and its love of comfort and pleasure, that class is coextensive with one of the three enemies of Christian life. We are dedicated without reserve, by our Baptism and incorporation in Christ, to fight the world, the flesh and the devil. And if we were born and brought up as bourgeois, then for us the middle class *is* the world—the first and in some ways the most difficult of our three enemies.

We have all been born with many handicaps. And the fact of being bourgeois is not something we get rid of in Baptism, like original sin. On the contrary, it is something that begins to grow on us along with our intellectual and spiritual life. It is a fungus that fixes on our souls and develops with them and at their expense and chokes out the growth of real Christianity, the true love of God.

Nevertheless it is no use to erect the notion of the middle class into a scapegoat from which we can stand back and detach ourselves in our own imaginations and upon which we can heap a certain amount of abuse without in fact doing anything to clean the worldliness out of our own actual, individual souls. After all, if we do that we are only favoring the disease that is in us instead of curing it because, as has just been said, one of the characteristics of that disease is the facility with which it evades responsibility by substituting fictions for realities.

There is no need to remind ourselves how, instead of helping and loving one another as Christians should, we follow the current of our society and give money to an organization that feeds a multitude of anonymous ciphers at the other end of the earth and then seek some outlet for our human feelings by going down to the movies and weeping over the death of the heroine's grandmother. There is no need to remind ourselves how we evade the responsibility of thinking by turning on a radio and letting a commentator deafen us with statements. We are generally well enough aware of the vices we share with the whole society of our time. The danger comes in when we try to escape from the world to the Church, but only succeed in making of our conversion another bourgeois evasion. It is all too easy to take all our middle-class mentality to church with us where, instead of throwing off the old man, the old bourgeois, we simply give him a new name and then light a candle and pray happily for his success.

In the six hundred years or so in which the Catholic Church has had to exist in a world dominated by the middle class there has been a little infiltration of its evils into some cells of the Mystical Body. That is not surprising. Christ, like the husbandman in the parable, foresaw from the start that cockle would be scattered in the good wheat by "an enemy" and He determined to "let both grow until the harvest." The very necessity of a reaction on the part of the healthy members of His Body who would be compelled to resist this infiltration in themselves and in their neighbors would all contribute to the sanctity of the Church. And so the evil influence might after all be an occasion of good. The thing for us to do, then, is to realize the real evil and react against it. And the first thing to recognize is that we will be tempted constantly to fight windmills and load our sins upon scapegoats and evade reality behind a screen of fictions and substitutions, and thus to end up where we started.

Nevertheless, it is a great thing to be enlightened at least to the point of realizing that the middle-class mentality is a spiritual evil and that it is Christ's enemy and a spiritual poison, provided we keep it on the concrete plane and do not divorce it entirely from the concept of our own worldliness which is the bourgeois spirit operating in us.

It is one of the most apparent misfortunes of the Church in our century to have become almost identified in certain minds with the middle class as if the interests of the Church were identical with those of the *bourgeoisie*. That identification is impossible because opposites cannot be identified. It is like saying Christ casts out devils by Beelzebub, the prince of devils. But since in actual fact so many Catholics live lives that are, for them, a practical identification of these two opposites, the idea prevails in the camp of Christ's worst enemies that Catholicism is, indeed, nothing but a front for the *bourgeoisie*.

There is no answer to this argument except the practical one of Christian perfection, sanctity. The tree has to be proven by its fruits, and the thing that so many of us seem to forget is that the communists have a right to demand that we show fruits worthy of Christ's doctrine. No one is so naive as to suppose that they would fall in love with us if we were the kind of Christians we are supposed to be; they probably would hate us even more. But the fact remains that for too many of us Christian perfection has been lost and obscured in a vague cloud of bourgeois fictions and evasions and therefore our lives are not, in fact, Christian, no matter how much we may endeavor to console ourselves with a few exterior formalities and gestures. *Populus hic labiis me honorat; cor autem eorum longe est a me.*

The impact of the *bourgeoisie* on Christianity has had the same characteristic features as its impact on every other department of life. It has produced a huge network of evasions and substitutions all around the fringe of Christianity. It cannot affect the essence of Christianity itself because the world cannot touch the heart of the Church. But it can certainly defile her garments. And thus the bourgeois spirit tends to work its way into Catholicism in order to get rid of the real thing and replace it by a cheap imitation. The purpose of this is the usual one: *to evade the trouble of leading a complete, integral Catholic life* by substituting sentiment for virtue, emotion for charity, formalities for prayer and exterior gestures for self-denial and sacrifice.

The centuries dominated by the middle class have seen a progressive degeneration of Catholic art, liturgy, music, architecture, and all the other exterior aids to spirituality which human talent can offer.

Now since the contemplative life and contemplative prayer are so close to the heart of Christianity and so intimately connected with Christian perfection it is inevitable that the middle-class mentality should subject them both to special treatment. Once again, it is the same old business of evasion and substitution. Take contemplation and empty it of all reality and all vital energy and offer up the empty shell, the dry husk instead of the real thing. The Holy See has had to condemn several of these substitutes of which the most dangerous, in itself, is the heresy of quietism.

Quietism is not, of course, an exclusively middle-class product. There is a certain instinct for inertia in fallen human nature. We tend of ourselves towards an ideal of rest which excludes all effort and all expense of thought or of desire. This is characteristic of Oriental mysticism which is really not contemplation at all. Since the love of comfort and the hatred of effort are fundamental to the bourgeois spirit it is scarcely surprising that quietism should have taken root in the Europe of the middle class.

But we cannot understand the vices of the substitute if we know nothing about the genuine article. True contemplation is a gift of God produced in the soul by the infused virtues and the gifts of the Holy Ghost, especially understanding and wisdom. It is itself nothing else but an experience of God revealing Himself to us in the intimate embrace of a love so pure that it overwhelms every other affection and excludes everything from our souls but the knowledge of Love alone. In the words of Saint Bernard, *Qui amat, amat et aliud novit nihil.*

The union of the soul with God in contemplation is effected in the depths of a holy darkness in which the intellect is blinded by excess of light and in which the natural powers of man, reduced to incapacity by the actual contact of an object Who is Infinite, are elevated and transported above the human level. In terms of human experience the early stages of contemplation seem like inactivity but that is far from true. On the contrary, the mind and will, blinded by darkness and aridity, are really being lifted to a degree of action that is far superior to anything our nature can comprehend. In fact, human nature has subordinated its function as the principle of these immanent operations and our faculties are now moved directly by God Himself.

So profound and complete and intense is the interior activity of the soul under the direction of God in contemplation that Saint John of the Cross does not hesitate to say that it is in mystical union that the soul *"attains to a true fulfillment of the first commandment,"* namely to "Love the Lord our God with our whole heart and our whole mind and our whole strength." Saint John's statement is a strong one but his explanation is no less strong and perfectly clear. It is, he says, only in infused contemplation that the energies of the soul are completely united in God without any possibility of wandering away to any other object. It is only in mystical union that it really becomes possible for us literally to concentrate our whole mind and heart and soul and strength upon God. Without it we can only love Him with a love that falls somewhere short of this perfection. In mystical union, and above all in the mystical marriage, we reach the summit of supernatural perfection on earth and attain the end for which we were brought into existence. For, as Saint John of the Cross says, *"it was for the goal of this love that we were created."* It is a goal which most of us, unfortunately, never reach until we get to heaven. But at any rate it brings with it the full expansion and perfection of all our faculties and all our natural and supernatural gifts in the one work which is supreme and transcends every other—that of loving God with the same love by which He loves Himself.

The way to this love is a path of labor and effort and sacrifice. It means striving to detach ourselves from everything that is not God. It means not only withdrawing from the pleasures and ambitions of the world but even from the highest and most perfect natural activities of the mind and will. To the pure contemplative even the intuitions and reasoning of the metaphysician and the speculative theologian can, under certain circumstances, be a temptation and he must then put them aside as not good enough for him, and keep his eyes fixed on a higher ideal that is baffling because it is incomprehensible. Even the desire for the consolations of prayer and the ardor of sensible love and felt enthusiasm can be an obstacle to the soul's advance to union with God in the cloud of darkness. The way of contemplation demands the most complete and irrevocable sacrifice of everything that human nature could possibly prize and desire. It is a narrow way—so narrow that few are willing to enter upon it, or stay on it when they find out how narrow it actually is.

Contemplation costs so much that it offers itself as one of the most obvious subjects for bourgeois evasion. And quietism certainly did a good job of it. On the surface, quietism looks a little like contemplation. The faculties do, indeed, renounce their natural activity. The soul does remain empty and dark. It does enjoy a kind of rest. But the rest is not the peace of contact with God, it is nothing but the natural repose of inactivity. This is not the sleep in which the bride sings that her "heart watcheth"—*Ego dormio sed cor meum vigilat*—it is simply the sleep of a corpse or the trance of someone who had been drugged or hypnotized.

The emptiness and darkness of quietism are void indeed because there is nothing behind them: they are the emptiness and darkness of the abyss. This is not the blessed night, the *vere beata nox* of which the Church sings on Holy Saturday, it is the darkness that is properly called stygian, overshadowed by the wings of the demon.

And so, in fact, quietism is as opposed to true contemplation as hell is to heaven. Instead of being the perfection of pure love quietism denies and annihilates and refuses and abjures all love. It banishes and excludes all movement of desire, all hope of union, all tendency to seek God as our fulfillment and our reward. With the cessation of all effort and all desire comes the repudiation of virtue, prayer, sacrifice. The extreme quietists went so far that they thought it was even an act of great imperfection and "self-will" to trouble their complete inertia of soul by resisting temptation. For all these things the Church has had to condemn them.

In a way, quietism is the triumph of the bourgeois spirit. It has carried all the evasions to their logical extreme by evading *everything*. It has turned all the values of Christianity inside out and it has done so in the name of sanctity and Christian perfection. It has discovered that the supreme sacrifice is to give up even sacrifice itself. It has found out that the purest love is not to love at all. It has made love pure by annihilating the loving subject altogether and thus, in the name of love, it has rejected all love and made of it an imperfection and a sin.

It was certainly a convenient creed, this cult of utter inertia. All the unpleasant and difficult things about Christianity, all that nasty business about taking up the Cross—it was all found to be not only unnecessary but even "less perfect." It could now be looked upon as a vulgar and "human" effort at virtue to which this new mode of total annihilation was infinitely superior because it was so much more spiritual. In fact it was more than angelic, it was divine.

The bourgeois apostles of this heresy made a typical appeal to the members of their class when they asserted, with Mme. Guyon, that they had discovered a "quick way," an "easy way" to God. And yet it is not altogether easy to be a pure quietist either. Although we tend to inertia our minds and imaginations can never rest in themselves alone and therefore it requires a peculiar effort and discipline just to keep your mind empty and inactive. In spite of yourself activities and desires keep crowding in. In spite of yourself you find that you tend to seek rest not in nothing but in God, and commit the imperfection of doing things to please Him. And so pure quietism never appealed to very many disciples.

Semi-quietism has had much more success and the fact is that in practice it is much more convenient an error. In the first place it does not have the drawback of being extreme; and your bourgeois is afraid of extremes. Semi-quietism is nice and comfy and contains all the evasion of difficulties that the middle class could possibly desire without demanding an "emptiness" and an "annihilation" that would themselves imply some kind of concentration and effort. In fact, what semi-quietism boils down to in practice is this: you lead a comfortable life, denying yourself nothing that you really want and only taking care to avoid the sins that would really upset your life in a social way. You do not make too much effort to get out of bad habits which you cherish, you say, because they are so valuable in keeping you "humble." You "sanctify" everything with an act of pure intention, which means that you do whatever you like, but first pronounce a little formula dedicating the act to God. Of course you take good care not to develop any such thing as a tender conscience, examination of which might reveal that God did not really want these selfish acts that were dedicated so glibly to Him. And in any case it is too much bother to keep repeating and renewing your formula since you have found out that it is quite sufficient just to make the offering once a day—if you remember to do so while ambling down to breakfast and enjoying the sweet smell of fried eggs and hot rolls. Meditation? Contemplation? They all boil down to the same thing: you spend fifteen minutes with a blank mind, allowing distractions to pour through you without let or hindrance, without any desire to love or know or find God. But in any case, those fifteen minutes are apt to take a less and less frequent part in your life since you find that contemplation is much more easy and effective in a rocking chair with a pack of cigarettes and a picture magazine.

And still, perhaps one shouldn't complain: it is no small thing in the world we live in that there should actually be some people left who know that meditation and contemplation exist at all.

However, there are many different forms of laziness to which human nature is attracted under the guise of virtue. There is another way to evade the responsibilities and efforts implied by a deep interior life. And this temptation also makes many victims in America. It seems to be a far call from quietism. In fact, many fall into it on the pretext of getting away from quietism which they openly despise.

You know the type. He is a busy, active person. His imagination works overtime and keeps him jumping from project to project and ambition to ambition. He would like to lead a deep interior life. He has read a lot of books about it and can talk about mystical contemplation with a certain facility. But when it comes to subjecting himself to the long, obscure process of interior mortification and purification that a deep interior life demands, he seizes any excuse to run away. For him activity is a refuge. He flies to it at every possible opportunity, to get away from the specter of that dry darkness in which God would perhaps come too close and make too many demands and begin to strip him of himself and leave him in all his poverty and helplessness and fear.

It does not matter whether you evade the responsibilities of a contemplative vocation by too much activity or too little; in the end it is the same laziness and the same evasion. The substitute may only be something less good, not an outright evil. But if God wants you—as perhaps He wants many—to find perfection through a close union with Him in prayer, you will do a great disservice to yourself and to the Church and will show no little ingratitude to God if you too carelessly allow yourself to be drawn off into one of these evasions. And yet the danger is immeasurably great in a time when the spirit of materialism, the middle-class spirit, still pervades everything, where it has not already begun to give way to a more atrocious spirit still. For the materialism of the communist, as far as the intellectual and spiritual life is concerned, retains all the most deadening elements of the *bourgeoisie*. The revolutionary impetus does, it is true, attract a few minds with a certain vitality in them but wherever the "Party" gains power, everything spiritual and intellectual congeals into a mass of sickening ugliness and mediocrity beside which the worst outrages of bourgeois culture can claim a certain charm.

For us there remains one duty: the evasion of all these evasions and the discovery of reality. The simplest way is the way that was taken by Saint Francis of Assisi. Born of a bourgeois father and brought up in the bosom of the early *bourgeoisie*, Saint Francis had only one answer to the claims of his class and his culture when they made their inevitable attempt to frustrate his vocation. He stripped himself of every shred of clothing his father had given him and walked out into the world naked. His example was without doubt providential. Francis' longing to be identified with everything the middle class hates with an unutterable loathing was given us by God as the clear and unequivocal path by which we too can leave our "people and our father's house" and begin to travel the quickest road to sanctity.

And the middle class has realized this all too well. We all know how it has got even with the Poor Man of Assisi. In fact all the bad art and all the bad verse and all the rest of the appalling junk that has accumulated around the true Saint Francis and almost entirely obscured him from view has been a very effective reply to his attack.

We love to call him the *Poverello* because it makes poverty seem so quaintly remote and picturesque and it somehow reminds us of the days between wars when we went whirling through Assisi on a Cook's tour. We love to think of him preaching to the birds and perhaps it is because a congregation of birds brings with it not the slightest burden of responsibility.

There is only one way to break through the whole tissue of middle-class deceits with which we are surrounded from our birth and with which we tend to surround ourselves even more as we go on. We cannot compromise with our bourgeois heritage because compromise is its own game and we cannot meet the world on its own ground.

As long as we retain anything about us that we have received from the *bourgeoisie* the world will have some kind of a claim on us. We must do what Saint Francis did: strip ourselves of everything and run away naked. And that means a very real, not merely metaphorical interior and exterior poverty: a poverty that involves hardship and suffering and hunger and privation and blind dependence on God. The way to perfection was marked out clearly enough by Jesus Christ Who, when a rich young man refused His call to perfection, remarked to His disciples: "It is easier for a camel to pass through the eye of a needle than for a rich man to enter into the Kingdom of Heaven." But always remember that in the Gospel of Christ the negative ascetic element is only one side of the coin. For to those who left all things He always promised not only "treasure in heaven," and "life everlasting" but even on earth that hundredfold reward which the Fathers of the Church recognized in the joys of contemplation.

The Contemplative Life:
Its Meaning and Necessity

The Dublin Review was the earliest continually published Catholic periodical in the English-speaking world, having been founded in 1836 by the Irish statesman Daniel O'Connell and Nicholas Wiseman, the future English cardinal, whose article in an early issue of the *Review* would have a profound effect on John Henry Newman's journey toward Rome. Despite its title, chosen to suggest to readers a major center of Catholic culture in the British Isles, throughout its long life the periodical was actually published in London. It continued in existence until 1969, when it merged with the English Jesuit magazine *The Month*. Merton's article in this prestigious journal appeared in issue 446 (Winter 1949): 26–35, his first original periodical publication outside the United States. Beginning as it does with a summary of the sudden, unexpected expansion of Cistercian monasticism in America, that bastion of busyness and activism, the article gives the impression of being a kind of report on the contemplative life from a trans-Atlantic perspective. Merton explains the upsurge in interest in contemplation, within and beyond monasteries, as the consequence of a widespread disillusion with contemporary society in the wake of the devastation of the Second World War, and he even cites the influence of existentialism as evidence of an awareness of spiritual darkness and emptiness that at least potentially recognizes a need for contemplation. His statement that "it is the function of contemplation to penetrate this interior darkness and walk by faith upon the void of the abyss which is at the center of all meaning" features language that he would use once again toward the end of his life in *The Climate of Monastic Prayer*

and other late writings. Most of the article, however, is written in
the more traditional terminology of the scholastics, Aquinas in
particular, and draws a sharp distinction between authentic
Christian contemplation and "the various mysticisms of the
Orient," which Merton dismissively considers as appealing to a
desire for spiritual autonomy and as expressing a sort of nihilistic
scorn for a sick world. It should be noted, however, that very
shortly after this article appeared, Merton's attitude toward the
East began to undergo a profound change. He writes in a journal
entry for January 26, 1950, "Msgr. Sheen sent us another special
edition of the *Études Carmelitaines*. . . . But in this issue of the
Études are many exciting things, including an article on Hindu
mysticism by a Swami, which makes me regret all the rash
judgments I ever made of Hindu mysticism. It is surprising how
much Yoga has in common with St. Bernard—at least in the
psychology of mysticism. Self knowledge is the first step in the
ascent. The problem of liberating our deeper energies from base
preoccupations which enfeeble and dissipate them" (*Entering the
Silence*, 402). In the body of the article, Merton corrects common
misapprehensions about the contemplative life, many of which
he had touched on in previous articles as well. He points out that
authentic contemplation, rooted in charity, is "essentially social,"
a foretaste of the everlasting unity of all the redeemed in and
through union with God. He stresses that this unity is already
expressed and experienced through prayer as well as through
action that is the fruit of this prayer (a topic already considered
in "Active and Contemplative Orders" and to be revisited in
"The Primacy of Contemplation," published shortly afterward).
He refutes the claim that contemplation is more emotional than
intellectual and maintains with Aquinas that it fulfills the intellectual life by transcending it. He concludes by declaring that a
commitment to contemplation on the part of a substantial number of Christians has the potential to spark a spiritual revolution
that could bring peace to the world, then leaves his readers to
envisage for themselves the grim alternative.

There are six Trappist monasteries in the United States. Soon
there will be seven. And if the Trappist monks had enough trained

men to start other new foundations there would soon be many more, because day after day new offers come in to the Superiors of this strict contemplative Order requesting that colonies of monks be sent to every part of the United States.

Of the six monasteries that are already flourishing in Kentucky, Iowa, Rhode Island, Georgia, Utah and New Mexico, two are a hundred years old, one is fifty years old and the other three were founded within the last five years. The two oldest abbeys had a terrible struggle for the first fifty or sixty years of their existence. Trappist Superiors in Europe, seeing that there were practically no American vocations to the silent, contemplative cloisters of the monks, were almost convinced that the contemplative life was impossible in America. Americans were too active, too restless. They were too fond of comfort and recreations. They had to talk or burst. You could never keep them quiet and pin them down to lives of austere penance and spiritual poverty, lives concentrated upon the union of the intellect and the will with God in the obscure and purifying light that is infused, by the Holy Spirit, into the souls of the saints!

Yet now, since World War II, all the Trappist monasteries in the States are crowded to the doors with young Americans, vigorous and happy men, with all the energy and the common sense and good-humor and sociability that characterize that nation. In a way, it almost amounts to a spiritual revolution. It is something that will have its repercussions on thousands of Americans who would never seriously think of becoming monks, and yet for whom the contemplative life may well turn out to be a matter of vital importance.

The contemplative life, in its purest and strictest sense, is led in monasteries. But in a broader sense every life can be dedicated to some extent to contemplation, and even the most active of lives can and should be balanced by a contemplative element—leavened by the peace and order and clarity that can be provided by meditation, interior prayer, and the deep penetration of the most fundamental truths of human existence.

The fact is that America seems to be waking up to the need of just some such thing as this. People are obscurely becoming aware of the truth that "with desolation is the whole world made desolate because there is no one that thinketh in his heart."

The collapse of the vague materialistic humanism that has been common currency for the past two or three centuries has left the world tragically aware of its own spiritual bankruptcy. Generation after generation of men have so lost the sense of an interior life, have so isolated themselves from their own spiritual depths by an exteriorization that has at last ended in complete superficiality, that now we are scarcely capable of enjoying any interior peace and quiet and stability. Men have come to live so exclusively on the surface of their being that life has become a mere quest of rudimentary pleasures and a flight from physical and mental pain. We are left at the mercy of external stimuli, and stimulation has even come to take the place that used, at one time, to be occupied by thought and reflection and understanding. Even religion has degenerated, in some quarters, into a cult of feelings and pious emotions and, at best, a vague sense of fellowship and kindness and general optimism about one's neighbor. We fall pitifully in love with whatever flatters us, and our existence becomes a perpetual search for whatever comforts our over-excitable sensibilities. Under such conditions, interior peace, which must necessarily depend on a certain moral stamina, and on resistance to useless stimulation, has become, for most men, absolutely impossible.

In consequence of all this, when our world collapses on our heads—as it is trying very hard to do at this moment—we have no way to react except to make more and more noise, deafen ourselves with arguments that have little or no meaning, until at last we fold up and retreat into the silence of dumb despair.

The spiritual bankruptcy of man has left him no refuge within himself, no interior citadel to which he can withdraw to collect his strength and size up the moral situation that confronts him, and in which he can come to some decision as to where to turn for help. Indeed, the last place in the world where the modern man seeks refuge or consolation is in the depths of his own soul. We know too well that our souls are empty, gutted, ruined structures. We would no more think of taking up residence within ourselves than we would of living in a haunted house.

Most people do not realize the real source of their terror. The fact is, however, that if you descend into the depths of your own spirit, of your own metaphysical actuality, and arrive somewhere near the center of what you *are*, you are confronted with the inescapable truth that, at the very roots of your existence, you are in constant and immediate and inescapable contact with the infinite power of God Who is Pure Actuality and Whose creative and personal will keeps you, every moment, in existence. And this is the one thought that most men seem to be so anxious to avoid.

Strangely enough, modern philosophy has not altogether feared to confront the metaphysical emptiness which is the subjective center of a soul that is spiritually lost. The cosmic despair of the existentialist has something of truth in it, because it is a reflection of the existentialist's own interior life. What is more, the darkness and the void which the existentialist apprehends within himself as a matter of experience is apt to be, in all truth, the experience of an absolutely unknown and transcendent and unfriendly God: the experience of the God Whom we cannot know because He has uttered against us the terrible judgement, "Amen, I know you not."

It is not surprising, therefore, that the existentialists have made such capital of the writings of a profoundly religious man, the Danish Protestant mystic Kierkegaard, for whom this cosmic anguish was a terrible reality. One feels that the existentialist who is absolutely honest and true to his own examination of himself is likely to find himself suddenly on the road to a conversion that will show him that the void, which he cannot exorcise by rationalization, can quickly become charged with an infinite meaning and reality, under the influence of that imponderable and mysterious power called grace.

Now it is the function of contemplation to penetrate this interior darkness and walk by faith upon the void of the abyss which is at the center of all meaning.

Perhaps that sounds very esoteric and very frightening. It should not. On the contrary, it should be very comforting, because it means that the contemplative life is founded on the simplest and most fundamental of all virtues: the theological virtue of faith.

What is contemplation? What is the contemplative life?

The broadest definition of contemplation is given by St. Thomas as the simple, comprehensive view of truth (*simplex intuitus veritatis*). It is the deep, penetrating view of a truth, embracing all its essentials in a glance, and resting in a profound absorption that savors all the meaning and reality of that truth, without discursive activity in the mind. In the strict sense, contemplation is a gaze that penetrates not just any truth, but the Truth of God as He is in Himself, as reason can never know Him, and as He is made manifest directly to us in the illumination of a divine gift which nature can do nothing to acquire.

The contemplative life is simply a life in which everything is ordered to the union of the mind and will with God in this perfect love of truth.

Contemplation is the fullness of the Christian life. It is the deep and supernatural and perfect experience of God, which we were all created to enjoy in heaven and which those who listen to God, on earth, and make the sacrifices which He asks of them, may taste even before they enter into heaven: *quaedam inchoatio vitae aeternae* (a certain beginning of eternal life—St. Thomas).

It may perhaps come as a secret disappointment to the modern non-Catholic to find out that contemplation is so completely and so traditionally Christian and that it is inseparably connected with the pursuit of spiritual perfection. Sanctity is no more popular today than it has been for the past five centuries. To the average secular human being, the odor of sanctity is scarcely more pleasant than the odor of mothballs or of old attics where things have been left to molder and where the rats have made their nests. If being a contemplative involves at least trying to be a saint, they will have nothing to do with it. The reason for that is, principally, that they do not want to arrive at an insight into truth that is not acquired by their own powers—one to which they have to be raised by God's grace at the cost of an intense and uncompromising interior purification.

One suspects that half the people who are curious about contemplation today are looking for spiritual excitement and for experiences that will satisfy an innate, egotistic craving to be something more than the general run of men. That is perhaps one reason why Oriental mysticism is still more popular with intellectuals than the mysticism of Christ and of Christian tradition. The Gospel has been preached to everybody, but very few people can tell you the distinction between the different varieties of Buddhism. Also, when all is said and done, the various mysticisms of the Orient offer the appearance of teaching an infallible method, a discipline which will put the most sublime contemplation within the reach of the man who can work out the secret of controlling muscles and nerve-reactions which are, in most men, involuntary and instinctive. If contemplation is arrived at by superhuman self-control and by a supreme and subtle and intense application of intellect and will, it offers, indeed, a considerable appeal to our appetite for self-glorification. In fact, to become a Yogi and to be able to commit moral and intellectual suicide whenever you please, without the necessity of actually *dying*, to be able to black out your mind by the incantation of half articulate charms and to enter into a state of annihilation in which absolutely nothing is known or hoped for or desired, in which all the faculties are inactive and the soul is as inert as if it were dead—all this may well appeal to certain minds as a refined and rather pleasant way of getting even with the world and with society, and with God Himself for that matter. It makes it possible for one to reply to all the wars, all the misery and degradation of our world, as well as to all its claims upon our conscience, with a huge ontological snub. It gives one the sense that one has told the whole universe to go and jump into a metaphorical lake. But, unfortunately, this is not supernatural contemplation. It is not the contemplative life, and it does nothing to perfect or to sanctify the soul of a man in the truly supernatural order; although without doubt the ascetics of the East, being probably, on an average, as sincere and honest as anyone dedicated to what he conceives to be an ideal can be, do sometimes achieve a certain natural perfection which is perfect enough to make many men in our civilization—religious people included—look rather silly.

The contemplative life necessarily implies asceticism and withdrawal, recollection, interior peace. To use the traditional Christian terms, it depends essentially on renunciation and self-sacrifice.

It means "giving up the world." It means withdrawing at least morally, if not physically, from the confusion and unrest that prevail in a society dedicated to the cult of power and pleasure and wealth, not to mention cruelty, violence, degradation.

Since the contemplative life implies an uncompromising denial and rejection of all the values which most people in the world actually live by, it is generally called anti-social. That is manifestly false. The contemplative life, in the Christian sense, is essentially *social*. The chief nourishment and source of Christian contemplation is precisely the liturgy, which is a communal activity of worship, social by its very nature, centered upon certain social "signs" or Sacraments, the chief of which, the Holy Eucharist, or the Body and Blood of Christ, is the *Sacramentum unitatis*, perfecting the union of all the faithful with one another and with God in one love and in the Mystical Body of Christ. Those who dedicate themselves by vow to the contemplative life in religious communities find themselves leading the most strictly communal and social kind of life it would be possible to imagine, and the last man who should be accepted in a contemplative monastery is a misanthrope! If you are anti-social by temperament, for pity's sake never enter a Trappist monastery: you will go crazy in ten minutes.

The final perfection and culmination of the contemplative life is the union of the saints with God in heaven, and no one who has read St. Augustine's *City of God* can question for an instant the social and communal character of the contemplative city of the blessed! An English Cistercian monk of the twelfth century, Baldwin of Canterbury, summed up the teaching of the Augustinian tradition on this point in his tract *De Vita Coenobitica* (On the Common Life), in which he started from the typically Pauline thesis that the contemplative life of men and angels is a participation in the inner, contemplative life of God Himself, One in Three Persons, and that, since the life of the Holy Trinity is essentially social, our contemplation will itself be more perfect in proportion as it enters more deeply into the communion which unites the Father and the Son in One Spirit. "Where there is perfection of love there must be perfect sharing, perfect communion" (*ubi plena est dilectio, plena est communio*). Hence it is the function of the Christian, contemplative community on earth to imitate and reflect the perfect union of love and peace in heaven, where the elect unite in one canticle of wonder at the glory of the Truth Who has absorbed them all into His own tremendous Life. Contemplatives begin on earth to lead the life of that "most joyous and happy society of the citizens of heaven living together in common" (*jucundissima et felicissima societas supernorum civium communiter viventium*). St. Bernard of Clairvaux makes the perfection of the most perfect social virtue, fraternal charity, one of the normal and essential preparations for infused contemplation, in which the soul is united immediately to God. His basis is the principle laid down by St. John the Evangelist: "He that loveth not his brother whom he seeth, how can he love God, whom he seeth not?" (I John 4:20).

However, someone may argue that it seems to be an act of hatred rather than of love for men to withdraw into a contemplative community, or even to lead the contemplative life while remaining in the world, thus "leaving society to its own devices" without "doing anything positive" to help cure the evils which afflict it. This, too, is a fallacy. It ignores, first of all, the power of prayer and the influence of personal sanctity. Those who imagine that a contemplative monastery is, socially speaking, a useless luxury, implicitly (if not explicitly!) deny that prayer has any real influence in the life of the world and attach more importance to the efforts of men than to the intervention of God, when it comes to healing the wounds of which the society of our time is now nearly dead. But since ours has been an age of unparalleled activity, both religious and secular, and one in which every conceivable human effort and device has been brought to bear on the problems of our time, and with less and less success, it is surprising that even those who scorn the idea of prayer have not been tempted to consider that perhaps human wisdom and human good-will are not sufficient to save us from the hell our own five wits have created all around us! There is not much reason for arguing this point further. It is one that works itself out quite simply, as a matter of experience. It is becoming increasingly evident that the only men in the world who are really happy are the ones who know how to pray.

The power of prayer is not the only contribution a contemplative has to offer to society. There is something more. Contemplation, at its highest intensity, becomes a reservoir of spiritual vitality that pours itself out in the most telling social action. St. Thomas Aquinas holds that the only really effective teaching and preaching is that which flows from the fullness of contemplation: *ex plenitudine contemplationis derivatur* (*Summa Theologica*, II-IIae, q. 188, a. 6). But this does not mean that for St. Thomas contemplation is only a means to an end, and that it is ordered to something beyond itself, to social action. On the contrary, he asserts without equivocation that the contemplative life is by its very nature superior to the active life. Contemplation is the end of all human existence (*finis totius humanae vitae*) and fulfills all the highest potencies of the soul in supreme vision and perfect love. The act of contemplation, to which the contemplative life is ordered, is proper to those who have reached the highest perfection (*proprium perfectorum*). Consequently, the contemplative life is not ordered to the service of action, but vice versa, action is ordered to contemplation. The contemplative life, as such, is better than the active life. *Vita contemplativa simpliciter est melior quam activa* (*Summa*, II-IIae, q. 182, a. 1). And therefore even the religious Orders whose vocation it is to bring truth to men by writing, teaching, preaching, by the study and dissemination of philosophy and theology, are, in the eyes of St. Thomas, to be much more than mere "teaching orders." They are, by their very nature and institution, contemplative. I would not dare to insist on this point unless two modern Dominicans, who may be taken as official spokesmen for the great Order of Friars Preachers which has played so brilliant a part in the revival of Catholic learning in our time, had not explicitly repeated this assertion in the clearest possible terms. Fr. Garrigou-Lagrange, O.P., flatly denies that "the apostolic (i.e., preaching) life has apostolic action for its primary and principal end." He denies that contemplation is merely a secondary end in such a life, and asserts that the "apostolic life *tends principally to contemplation.*"[1] Fr. Joret, O.P.,[2] also tells us that the Friar Preacher does not apply himself to contemplation merely to store up material for his preaching and

---

[1] *The Three Ages of the Interior Life*, Vol. II, pp. 491–92.
[2] *The Dominican Life*, pp. 82–83.

teaching, but that contemplation is, for him, "a true end," to be sought "for its own sake," and the highest of all ends on earth. He adds that contemplation, far from being a simple means to a more fruitful apostolate, is "the summit of the apostolic life."

The intensely fruitful intellectual activity that has marked the greatest ages of the Catholic Faith is something that needs hardly to be recalled to mind here. No one can possibly deny the immense social value of the works of the great doctors of the Church, the Fathers of the East and West, St. Cyril of Alexandria or St. Augustine of Hippo; the great scholastics, St. Thomas, St. Bonaventure and the scholars, philosophers and theologians of later ages. But the greatness of the greatest of these, and the fruitfulness of their work, sprang principally from the fact that they were contemplatives and that their most cogent intuitions came to them not in study but in the high altitudes of contemplative prayer.

No one can sensibly assert, in view of all this, that the contemplative life is more emotional than intellectual and that it produces no fruit beyond the poetry that emanates from some personal experience that is essentially suspect because it cannot be checked by a psychologist, and which has to be relegated to the cloudy realms where religion associates with art and where nothing definite can be said about anything.

It is true that contemplation transcends the level of reason and of logical discourse. But, just as Christ came to fulfill the moral law, and not to destroy it, contemplation comes to *fulfill* the intellectual life of the philosopher or theologian, not to destroy it. Nevertheless, if theology and philosophy are to achieve the fulfillment that only contemplative prayer can give them, they must be prepared to relinquish their own characteristic method of procedure at least at the moment of contemplation. Human discourse, even at its most exalted level, crawls along the ground, when it is compared with the swift, dark, soaring flight of contemplation which pierces to the heart of truth like an arrow, transcending and surpassing all concepts and images that can be clearly grasped by the mind and losing itself in the blinding flash of an intuition that is dark through excess of light and obscures the mind at the moment of the most intense illumination. For the Gift of Understanding confounds all our faculties at the very peak of their fulfillment by a shaft of supernatural lightning. It is what St. John of the Cross called a "ray of darkness" (*un rayo de tinieblas*), quoting the Pseudo-Areopagite. The Gifts of the Holy Ghost, especially those of Understanding and Wisdom, by which contemplation is brought to its full maturity in the soul of the believer, are themselves developments of the theological virtues of faith, hope and love, and all these three transcend reason and the natural virtues of man, operating on an entirely supernatural level in which, as far as we can experience, our own faculties seem at first to be helpless. In fact, it is this sense of helplessness that usually baffles and discourages those who refuse to allow God to draw them any further into the ways of contemplation. And it is this element in the writings of contemplatives that leads others to condemn them as anti-intellectual. However, St. Thomas Aquinas and St. John of the Cross, together with all the great Catholic mystics, teach quite rightly that it is only in contemplation, and under the direct guidance of the Holy Ghost, that the human intellect and the human will reach their highest perfection. And they do so in a way that is utterly unfamiliar to human nature, for the light of contemplation and the fire of infused charity strike the intellect and will not from the outside, through the medium of sense images, like ordinary natural experience, but from within the very substance of the soul. And God illuminates the mind and draws the will to Himself by unifying them in the substance of the soul, in which they are rooted, and where our very being enters into immediate contact with Him Who is our Creator and Who sustains us every moment in existence.

Such, then, is the nature of contemplation. Far from being weird and esoteric, it is the traditional perfection and summit of the Christian life. Far from being anti-social, it is produced only in those souls that have begun to be absorbed in the infinite and uncreated Love Who is the only source of all social harmony and of justice and of peace. Far from being anti-intellectual, it is the only possible means by which the mind of man can be elevated to the vision of that infinite truth by which alone we can be satisfied.

This contemplation is not the work of men but the work of God. He will produce it in those whom His grace has first separated from the violence and greed and injustice and cruelty of the world, with all its noise and its shallow appeals to passion and its crass stupidity. He will produce it in the souls of men only as an answer to penance, renouncement and prayer. If we can muster up enough humility, by His grace, to make use of these three means, the world will be the scene of a tremendous religious revolution, and there will be peace. If not . . .

The Primacy of Contemplation

In an unpublished December 21, 1950, letter to his editor, Robert
Giroux, Merton wrote that he wanted the material excerpted
from his article "Active and Contemplative Orders" to be omitted
from the planned paperback edition of *The Seven Storey Mountain*.
(This was never done.) He added, "There has been a lot of
criticism of the theology involved here and I have restated the
whole position more clearly in an article which would be for that
collection of articles, if ever. . . ." The criticism, of course, was
primarily that of Fr. Fearon, OP, and the new article restating his
position was "The Primacy of Contemplation," published earlier
in the year in *Cross and Crown* 2, no. 2 (1950): 3–16, a quarterly
magazine begun the previous year by the Chicago Province of the
Dominicans (an appropriate venue), which in 1978 was renamed
Spirituality Today and continued under that title until it ceased
publication in 1992. Merton had evidently thought at the time
about writing an article responding directly to Fr. Fearon's
critique but was discouraged from doing so by Dom James Fox,
his abbot, and restricted himself to writing a letter to *The Thomist*;
for details see his February 10, 1949, letter to Jacques Maritain
(*Courage for Truth*, 24). The new article makes no mention of
either Merton's original piece or Fearon's rebuttal, but it is evident that Merton is covering much the same ground and coming
to much the same conclusions, while reformulating his case to
avoid the inaccuracies or unclear statements that had prompted
Fearon's negative strictures. Merton begins the essay by rooting
the traditional teaching on contemplation in the Scriptures, quoting passages from Paul's letters and John's gospel that, without
using the word, make clear that contemplation, participation in the

116

trinitarian life of love through union with the crucified and risen Christ, "is the reason for our existence." He tellingly notes that in the New Testament, preaching is presented as the means provided to lead individuals and the church as a body to the end of union with God. At this point he turns to Saint Thomas and declares that his teaching on Christian perfection is identical to what he himself has just summarized from Scripture. He carefully considers the Thomistic teaching on the "state of perfection" found in the religious life before going on to consider the related but not identical question of active and contemplative lives—a distinction Fearon had accused Merton of failing to make in his earlier article. He notes that Saint Thomas teaches that the contemplative life, living for God alone and loving God directly, is superior to the active life, though in concrete circumstances, because of the demands of charity, active works might be more in accord with the divine will than contemplative prayer would be. He is then able to move on to the point he really wants to make—the major point of his earlier article as well: that the "apostolic" life of preaching the Gospel is accounted the best by Thomas precisely because it overflows from and shares the fruits of contemplative union with God. Thus contemplation is not to be considered a means to the end of action but an end in itself that has as a consequence the communication of its experience of the divine light.

To support this principle that *"it is contemplation itself which is the primary and principal end of the apostolic life,"* Merton calls to witness the eminent Dominican theologians Reginald Garrigou-Lagrange and Ferdinand Joret, both of whom he had mentioned in his article for *The Dublin Review* a few months earlier, as well as another Dominican, Fr. M. V. Bernadot, the theologian Charles Journet, the rule of the Carmelites, and, to climax the discussion, the most distinguished contemporary Thomist philosopher, Jacques Maritain. In the two final paragraphs, in the context of Maritain's distinction between perfection fully acquired and perfection in the process of being acquired, Merton reiterates the conclusion he had made in "Active and Contemplative Orders," suggesting that if "one has not yet arrived at the contemplation whose fruits are to be shared with others . . . the silence of a Cistercian cloister, hidden in the depths of the country, the life of labor, vigils, fasting, penance and constant prayer, may prove to be a more favorable atmosphere for doing so than a college

campus in a busy modern city." He finally comes full circle by
touching on the very paradox that had sparked the discussion in
the earlier article, citing Maritain again as reconciling Pius XI's
assertion of the superiority of the contemplative life with the
Thomistic elevation of the apostolic life as the highest. In his final
words—"this is not the place to quarrel about the merits of religious orders in detail" and "in the abstract the preaching orders
have, and will always retain, the rank of highest dignity . . .
because they are *de jure* our greatest contemplatives"—Merton
reasserts the "primacy of contemplation" and implicitly defends
the position that he believed had been so misconstrued and
misrepresented when he had presented it previously in "Active
and Contemplative Orders."

The Christian life is a continual effort to achieve beatitude by
union with God, a union of love in which God is seen face to face,
as He really is. Everything else, every interest other than this one
consuming passion for God, is secondary. God Himself is the end
for which we have been created, and other things, other preoccupations can only be called important in so far as they help us to
arrive at union with Him. When they cease to bring us closer to
God, they become harmful. They have to be rejected, or else our
spiritual life will soon become stagnant, because the living stream
of charity will have ceased to carry us on toward our only end.

Jesus clearly told His disciples this, the night before His Crucifixion. He told them that eternal life was the knowledge of the one
true God and of Jesus Christ whom He had sent.[1] He told them
that this knowledge was arrived at by love, by obedience to His
will, by subjection to the guidance of the Paraclete, the Spirit of
Love, who proceeded from the Father and from the Son. This Spirit
of Love would inevitably separate them from the world in order
to unite them to the Word. For the Holy Spirit would come to
convince the world of "sin, of justice, and of judgment."[2] Since no
man could serve two masters, there was to be an irreconcilable
division between the world and Christ. The disciples of Christ,

[1] John 17:3.
[2] John 16:8.

who would arrive, through Him, at union with the Father in love and knowledge, must follow in His footsteps, carrying the cross. The Holy Spirit would demand this of them as a token of their divine sonship: "For if you live according to the flesh, you shall die: but if by the Spirit you mortify the deeds of the flesh, you shall live. For whosoever are led by the Spirit of God, they are the sons of God."[3] But all those who thus obeyed the Holy Spirit and fulfilled the will of Christ, would be filled with the "Spirit of Truth whom the world cannot receive because it seeth Him not nor knoweth Him; but you shall know Him because He shall abide with you and be in you."[4] And thus St. Paul can sum up the Christian vocation: "That all men may see what is the dispensation of the mystery which hath been hidden from eternity in God, who created all things: that the manifold wisdom of God may be made known . . . according to the eternal purpose which He made, in Christ Jesus our Lord." And the Apostle adds: "For this cause I bow my knees to the Father of our Lord Jesus Christ . . . that He would grant you, according to the riches of His glory, to be strengthened by His Spirit with might unto the inward man, that Christ may dwell by faith in your heart that, being rooted and founded in charity, you may be able to comprehend with the saints what is the breadth and the length and the height and the depth; to know also the charity of Christ, which surpasseth all knowledge, that you may be filled unto all the fullness of God."[5] The word "contemplation" is not found, in our modern sense, in the Gospels or in St. Paul. Nevertheless there is no higher contemplative ideal than the ideal of St. John or St. Paul. To be drawn by the Holy Spirit into union with the Word, Christ Jesus, and, by virtue of this divine adoption, to share in the infinite riches of life, vision, and love which are contained in the Holy Trinity: this is the Christian ideal. In its perfection, in the beatific vision it is a life of the highest contemplation. All Christian life is ordered to this contemplation of God in God. Contemplation is the reason for our existence.

[3] Rom. 8:13 f.
[4] John 14:17.
[5] Ephes. 3:9 f., 14–19.

Among the divinely ordained means to this end, is preaching. Preaching plays an essential role in the Christian economy. As the Father sent Christ so Christ sends His disciples into the world[6] to preach to all nations.[7] However, preaching remains a means to an end. The end is always the union of souls with God, the union of the Church with God in vision and love.

A great modern poet, Paul Claudel, gives simple and powerful expression to this fundamental truth when he says: "The great need of modern man is prayer, the interior life, the renewal, at any price, of our contact with God. We are all dying of hunger and thirst." And, anticipating the objections of many who believe that a deep interior life of prayer is something that only a few saints can dare aspire to, he continues: "We have the right and the duty to profit by the saints; we must not leave them to themselves. We must make use of their discoveries. . . . If we are to penetrate into the interior life we must not stand around looking at our own feet. We must fix our gaze upon the stars."[8]

What is the teaching of St. Thomas on Christian perfection? It is none other than that which we have just outlined. Every being is perfect in so far as it attains the end for which it was created. But the end for which man was created is union with God, by charity. Hence Christian perfection is measured by charity. The more we love God, the more closely are we united to Him and the more perfect are our lives.[9] The perfection of man is a complete and perfect union of all his powers and all his being with God: *ut totaliter Deo inhaereat.*[10] We are saints when we no longer live for ourselves but for God alone.[11]

In order to help men to arrive at this close union with God, the Church has instituted an exterior state of perfection, characterized by solemn, public dedication to the pursuit of this union. This state

---

[6] John 17:18.
[7] Matt. 28:19.
[8] *Présence et Prophétie*, p. 23, note.
[9] IIa IIae, q. 184, a. 1.
[10] *Ibid.*, q. 186, a. 1.
[11] Caritas proprie facit tendere in Deum, uniendo affectum hominis Deo ut scilicet homo non sibi vivat, sed Deo. *Ibid.*, q. 17, a. 6.

of perfection is what we call the religious state. By entering monasteries and convents, men and women try to subject themselves more closely to the influence of the Holy Spirit, retiring from the world and its legitimate satisfactions in order to give themselves more freely and more completely to the one thing that really matters: the search for God. Thus they strive to achieve the highest perfection that anyone can attain in this life—a perfection that is not absolute, that does not exclude every imperfect act, every human weakness, but that does exclude every habit which would prevent the total dedication of one's whole self to God.[12] Of course the fact that one is officially placed in a juridical "state" does not mean that one necessarily becomes interiorly perfect. One may become a greater saint outside the "state of perfection" than in it, although ordinarily we might expect the religious life to lead one more quickly and safely to union with God.

For instance, a secular priest would not be in what St. Thomas calls "the state of perfection" because he does not dedicate himself by vow to the priesthood. By reason of his ordination he would possess a far greater dignity than any member of a religious order who was not a priest, and he would also be bound to a greater holiness of life, although remaining, juridically, outside the "state of perfection."[13] Needless to say, in particular and concrete cases the secular priest might well find himself following a more heroic way of sanctity than a cloistered religious. But generically, and in the abstract, the religious state offers surer and more numerous means to advance in the life of union with God which is Christian sanctity.

Therefore, when he compares the religious and secular states, St. Thomas finds greater perfection in the religious life because it offers more protection against the dangers of the world and because it implies a more complete gift of one's self to God. He is applying the principles we have laid down. Perfection is measured by love. Love of God implies a desire to know God and to be united

---

[12] . . . ab affectu hominis excluditur non solum illud quod est caritati contrarium sed etiam omne illud quod impedit ne affectus mentis totaliter dirigatur in Deum. *Ibid.*, q. 184, a. 4.

[13] *Ibid.*

with Him, and this is impossible to anyone who does not leave behind the desires and ambitions of the world.

✠   ✠   ✠

Man's intellect is apt to act in two ways: it can seek truth in order to contemplate it, or it can seek truth as the norm of things to be done. Man can think practically or speculatively. According to this division of man's intellectual life, there are two broad ways of living open to us all.

We can devote ourselves to getting things done, producing effects outside ourselves, working for other men, serving society in a visible and tangible way. This is the active life. Or else we can devote ourselves principally to another mode of life which, though opposed to the active life, must not by any means be thought of as inert and unproductive. The contemplative life is certainly no less active than the active life. On the contrary, it is more "active" because its activity, being immanent and spiritual, is far superior to the bodily motion required for external works. The contemplative life is centered upon an act which is essentially intellectual but which is inseparably bound up with other acts of love from which it proceeds and by which it is perfected. This activity of knowing and loving is so close to the beatitude for which man was created that it tends to satisfy all our powers and that is why contemplation is described as "rest." In reality it is "restful" because it is so smooth and perfect, so satisfying to our whole being, that it is a prelude to the "rest" of heaven which will, nevertheless, be our supreme activity.[14]

However, it is not easy for fallen man to enter upon the ways of this superior activity. Our lives are so bound up with the activity of the senses that the interior discipline demanded by the life of contemplation is, to many, completely intolerable. They cannot

[14] Motus corporales exteriores opponuntur quieti contemplationis quae intelligitur esse ab exterioribus occupationibus, sed motus intelligibilium operationum ad ipsam quietem contemplationis pertinent. *Ibid.*, q. 180, a. 6, ad 1.

bear it, and they are forced to seek God in some spiritual landscape that has more familiar outlines. The desert is not for everybody. Some of us have to stay in the towns. Those who do so, in obedience to the Spirit of God, will find that their sanctity will in no way suffer, and they will discover that even in the active life there can and must be an element of contemplation.

St. Thomas asks himself the question whether there should be religious orders dedicated to the active life. His answer follows the lines we would expect. The key is, once again, charity. If the active life can lead man to a union of love with God, then it is fitting that religious orders should be devoted to works of the active life, for in that way they can serve their purpose of making saints. Now there is only one virtue of charity. The love of our neighbor is not a distinct virtue from our love of God. We love our neighbor for God's sake, and in view of God, and therefore fraternal charity is just as much a theological virtue as the love of God. In loving our brothers, we have God for our object. The works performed by religious in active orders are directed principally to God. They are works of divine charity. But this love for God is not exclusively and purely concerned with Him alone as is the contemplative's love for Him. Of course, we have to remember that there must be exterior activity and fraternal charity in the contemplative life just as there must be interior contemplation of God in the active life. This enters into St. Thomas's justification of the active life. Even in the case of what may, abstractly, be called the "purely active orders," St. Thomas says that their activity must be derived from contemplation at least in the sense that it is done in view of God.[15] But no man can be expected to direct all the activities of a busy day to God unless some part of that day is devoted to meditation and prayer and to exercise of the mind and will calculated to keep him aware of the presence of God and alive to the promptings of the Holy Spirit. The Holy Ghost must not only sanctify all our works but even perform them in us and for us, since it is God who

---

[15] Dum religiosi operibus vitae activae insistunt intuitu Dei, consequens est quod in eis actio ex contemplatione divinorum derivetur. Unde non privantur omnino fructu contemplativae vitae. *Ibid.*, q. 188, a. 2, ad 1.

worketh in us to will and to accomplish.[16] St. Thomas, therefore, clearly implies that religious in the active life have to lead lives of interior prayer.

Although, as we shall see, St. Thomas says that the contemplative life is generically superior to the active life, yet there are occasions when the active life can be more meritorious than the contemplative. What are these occasions? Simply those in which, accidentally, the active life represents a greater sacrifice, greater love for God, a purer intention, a more complete gift of one's self. St. Thomas uses the phrase *propter abundantiam divini amoris*.[17] True to his principles, he settles the question by an appeal to love, for where there is greater love there is greater perfection. But this concept of a *superabundant*, overflowing charity is one that recurs every time St. Thomas considers the value of leaving contemplation for action, and of preferring works to solitary union with God. It is very important to bear in mind that St. Thomas never said that one could become a saint by abandoning contemplation in favor of action if such a step implied a real lessening of the interior life, a diminution of charity, and a slackening of one's union with God. On the contrary, he was fully aware that a certain inherent weakness in human nature sometimes leads men to fling themselves into activity, under the pretext of charity, in order to escape the difficulties of an interior life that hangs heavy on their hands.

There is a passage in the *De perfectione vitae spiritualis*[18] in which the Angelic Doctor shows up the weaknesses of those who are attached to contemplation as well as of those who are active merely because they cannot be bothered to contemplate. Those who refuse to renounce the consolations of contemplative prayer, for a time, in order to serve the urgent spiritual interests of others, cannot

[16] Phil. 2:13.

[17] IIa IIae, q. 182, a. 2.

[18] Intendere saluti proximorum cum aliquo detrimento contemplationis propter amorem Dei et proximi, ad majorem perfectionem caritatis videtur pertinere quam si aliquis in tantum dulcedini contemplationis inhaereret quod nullo modo eam deserere vellet, etiam propter salutem aliorum . . . . Quae tamen perfectio caritatis in plerique proximorum utilitate vacantibus non invenitur, quos magis contemplativae vitae taedium ad exteriora deducit. *De perfectione vitae spiritualis*, c. 23.

claim that they are acting out of love: but St. Thomas adds that this fault is far less frequent than the opposite one, which he seems to think quite common.

✠   ✠   ✠

Comparing the active and contemplative lives, in the abstract, St. Thomas does not hesitate to give the primacy to contemplation. He says quite flatly that the contemplative life is, by its nature, generically, superior to the active life. *Vita contemplativa simpliciter est meliora quam activa.*[19] The active life is secondary. It is only the servant of contemplation, *magis servit vitae contemplativae quam dominetur.*[20] The contemplative life is more meritorious than the active life because the root of merit is the love of God and it is *per se* more meritorious to love God immediately, in Himself, than through our neighbor.[21] Although it may be an expression of great charity to devote oneself to patient toil for others, it is a far greater expression of love (*multo expressius signum*)[22] to abandon all the human satisfactions of this life in order to live for God alone in the nakedness of a faith that sometimes becomes extraordinarily bleak and arid to human nature. After all, if the labors of the apostolate are great, so are its consolations. It is very refreshing to see the results of one's efforts. It is pleasant to go out to the fields to bring in a rich harvest. Work itself, under such circumstances, becomes a consolation.

Does it seem like a great sacrifice to give up everything in order to serve the physical needs of the poor? Great indeed it is. But St. Thomas says that it is a greater and more pleasing sacrifice to give your whole soul to God in the darkness of contemplation and to lead other souls to do the same. Here are his words: "The more closely a man unites his own soul or the soul of another to God, the more pleasing is the sacrifice to God."[23]

---

[19] IIa IIae, q. 182, a. 1.
[20] *Ibid.*, ad 2.
[21] *Ibid.*, a. 2.
[22] *Ibid.*, a. 2, ad 1.
[23] *Ibid.*, a. 2, ad 2.

The ultimate reason for the primacy of the contemplative life, in the thought of St. Thomas, is that it is ordered to perfect charity. *Vita contemplativa non ordinatur ad qualemcumque dilectionem Dei sed ad perfectam.*[24] He brings this out in contrast to the charity demanded of the active life which, he says, is more common and less perfect than that demanded by the contemplative life. Thus the active life precedes contemplation *in via generationis* because the virtues of the active life must be practiced by all. They are the virtues that prepare the way for the higher reaches of prayer. But the charity of contemplatives is proper to the perfect, *proprium perfectorum.*[25]

One cannot argue that the pleasure of contemplation, being intellectual, is a purely selfish thing, a kind of refined, spiritual aestheticism. The contemplative's vision of God draws inspiration from love and leads to greater love. Indeed, it is only because the contemplative knows God better than others that he is able to love Him better. That is why, although the essence of contemplation is found in an act of the intellect, the end of contemplation is perfect love of God.[26] This term, this end, this perfection of love is so great that the contemplative loses himself entirely in God and not only hates himself by comparison with the beauty and truth that he beholds, but rather loses sight of himself altogether in order to seek and love God alone. The contemplative becomes so completely one with God in the act of contemplation that only God alone seems to exist and to act: as if there were no longer two beings but only One. Far from being selfish, this knowledge and love are the supreme renunciation of self, the *extasis* that empties a man out of himself into the infinite unselfishness of God.

Since St. Thomas describes perfection as a love so pure that it makes man live for God rather than for himself, and makes him belong totally and completely to God, it is easy to see why he calls the love which is the term of contemplation, proper to the perfect, *proprium perfectorum.* Need we add, once again, that St. Thomas's

---

[24] *Ibid.*, a. 4, ad 1.

[25] *Ibid.*

[26] Vita contemplativa non ordinatur ad qualemcumque dilectionem Dei sed ad perfectam. *Ibid.*

treatment of this question is purely theoretical and that in a concrete case it is quite likely that a Little Sister of the Poor or even a housewife in the world may arrive at this perfection while a Carthusian or Carmelite or Cistercian may remain far from it?

⊠   ⊠   ⊠

At the beginning of his *De doctrina Christiana* St. Augustine[27] says that if our contemplation of God, through Scripture, cannot be shared with others, it is not yet fully developed in us. If a good is of such a nature that it is not diminished by being shared, then, if we possess it without sharing it, we do not yet possess it in its perfection.

St. Thomas echoed that thought when he described the dignity of those religious orders which are devoted not only to contemplation but to the work of sharing the fruits of their contemplation with other men. The phrase used by the Angelic Doctor has become classical. *Sicut enim majus est illuminare quam lucere solum, ita majus est contemplata aliis tradere quam solum contemplari.*[28] St. Thomas concludes from this that the religious orders which are devoted to preaching and teaching are therefore superior to orders which are considered "purely contemplative" and that these in turn are superior to those which are called "purely active." But the fact that the preaching and teaching orders are accidently concerned with works of the active life does not make the active life *ipso facto* superior to the contemplative life. On the contrary, in the thought of St. Thomas, the activity of the preaching orders has a very special character. We remember that when St. Thomas agreed that the active life might be preferred to contemplation, in certain circumstances, he qualified his statement with the phrase, *propter abundantiam divini amoris.* When he comes to consider the activity of the apostolic orders, the same notion of superabundance is in the forefront of his mind. The dignity of the apostolic orders flows

---

[27] Omnis enim res quae dando non deficit, dum habetur et non datur, nondum habetur quomodo habenda est. *De doctrina Christiana*, I, 1. Migne, *P. L.*, 34, col. 19.

[28] IIa IIae, q. 188, a. 6.

from the fact that their preaching bears witness to the fullness of contemplation: *ex plenitudine contemplationis derivatur*.[29]

The dignity of the apostolic orders is not derived from their apostolate as such. It is not derived from their activity. It is not derived from their preaching. It is derived from their contemplation. The contemplation proper to the apostolic vocation is not simply a low degree of contemplation, but its *fullness*. The works to which these orders are devoted cannot be performed as they ought to be performed unless they are the overflow of contemplation in all its plentitude. And so, if St. Thomas considers the apostolic orders superior to merely contemplative orders, it is not because of what they accomplish in the external order of things. It is not because they get busy and *do* things that the Dominicans are to be preferred to the Carthusians, in the mind of St. Thomas. The only justification the apostolic orders can have for claiming superiority over the purely contemplative orders is the fact that they are destined, by their very nature, to the superabundance of contemplation—a contemplation that *has to overflow* and communicate itself to others.

St. Thomas does not take a merely abstract view of the conditions upon which the superiority of the apostolic orders depends, as if it were sufficient for the orders themselves to have a high ideal, while the interior lives of their members counted for nothing. Speaking in the same terms, using the image of a fire that burns and gives light, he speaks of preachers who, because they do not have deep interior lives of love and prayer, are lights in appearance only, and not in truth. They are light-bearers by vocation but in actual fact their lights have gone out—or else they were never lit. *Aliqui sunt lucernae solum quantum ad officium, sed quantum ad affectum sunt extinctae*.[30] The reason for this, says the Angelic Doctor, is that a spiritual light is not enkindled except by the fire of charity. He is speaking of the love which is the principle of contemplation. *Ardor praemittitur illustrationi*.[31]

---

[29] *Ibid.*
[30] *In Joan.* 5:35.
[31] *Ibid.*

Therefore, when St. Thomas argues that the preaching and teaching orders hold pride of place among all other religious institutes, he bases their dignity not merely on their activity but *on the contemplation which is the principle of that activity.* They owe their superiority to the fact that the very nature of their works implies a purer and more intimate love of God and a deeper, more experimental knowledge of His infinite goodness. Far from detracting from what he had said about the primacy of the contemplative life, St. Thomas' explanation of the superiority of the preaching orders only enhances the dignity of contemplation, which is the essential end of the apostolic vocation.

Let there be no hesitation on this point. The preaching and teaching orders are not destined merely to functions of the active life. The contemplative life is an absolutely essential end of the preaching vocation. Without it, the kind of preaching envisaged by St. Thomas will be impossible.

Nor is it sufficient to consider contemplation merely as a means to action, in the life of the preaching orders. According to Father Garrigou-Lagrange this would be a "diminution of the traditional teaching."[32] Contemplation is not a secondary end of the apostolic life. It is not the mere handmaid of activity. It does not take a subordinate rank to the work of preaching. On the contrary, *it is contemplation itself which is the primary and principal end of the apostolic life.* I am not making this up out of my own Cistercian head. I would never dare, of my own accord, to come out so flatly with such a statement, concerning the vocation of orders of which I have only a remote knowledge. I am simply quoting the most authoritative modern spokesman of one of the greatest of the preaching orders. Father Garrigou-Lagrange says quite clearly: "It is apostolic action itself which is *a means subordinated to the union with God* to which the apostle wishes to lead souls. . . . We must

---

[32] Some diminish the traditional teaching by saying that the apostolic life has apostolic action for its primary and principal end, but that it also tends toward a certain contemplation as a means necessary for action. *The Three Ages of the Interior Life*, II, 491.

say that *the apostolic life tends principally to contemplation* which fructifies in the apostolate."[33]

Nor is Father Garrigou-Lagrange alone in this opinion. Father Joret, O.P., in his quasi-official guide to the Dominican life, insists that the Friar Preacher does not merely use contemplation as a source for apostolic ideas. Contemplation is the very summit of the Dominican life, the highest of ends for the Friar Preacher. Contemplation and action are not two distinct ends of the apostolic life, of which the first is the means to the second. On the contrary, there is one end only: a contemplation so superabundant that it overflows in apostolic action.[34]

Father Bernardot, O.P., writes in a similar vein: "If the religious applies himself to prayer and study, not principally for the sake of contemplation itself, but in view of some active work, in order to be able to teach and to preach, his application to contemplation then *reduces itself to a work of the active life because it is performed chiefly in view of an exterior action.*"[35] It would follow that prayer and study, performed with an exterior activity in mind as their proximate end, would become works of the active life and would thus be inferior to works of the purely contemplative life. Msgr. Journet, writing in *La vie spirituelle*, remarks that:

> The apostolic life which involves exterior activity in the world is more excellent than the contemplative life *only in so far as its exterior activity, instead of preying upon contemplation as a parasite, is merely added to contemplation in order to manifest it.* As long as exterior activity attenuates the lustre of hidden contemplation, then the active life prevails, and *this active life is inferior both to the contemplative life and to the apostolic life.* What we call the apostolate, in ordinary parlance, is, quite often, nothing but the active life, and that in its lowest degree.[36]

---

[33] *Ibid.*, p. 492. Cf. *Salmanticenses, XX, De statu religioso*, Disp. II, dub. iii.

[34] Cf. *The Dominican Life*, pp. 82 f.

[35] Quoted in C. Journet's comments on *Umbratilem* in *La vie spirituelle*, October, 1927, p. (53).

[36] *Ibid.*

The Carmelites have an extraordinarily strict and lofty ideal in this respect. The primacy of contemplation is so jealously safeguarded in the Carmelite Rule that it can be said to be the essential characteristic of that Rule. So strictly is action subordinated to contemplation, in the Carmelite ideal, that without contemplation a Carmelite is not supposed even to attempt to enter the apostolate.[37]

✠   ✠   ✠

In closing, I can only refer the reader to the luminous pages of *The Things that are not Caesar's* in which Jacques Maritain has discussed our topic, the pre-eminence of contemplation.[38]

Here, M. Maritain makes a very important and sagacious distinction between two orders of perfection. There is perfection considered as fully acquired, and there is another perfection which is still in the acquiring. There are those who are still on their way to perfection and those who have, in a certain sense, arrived. St. Thomas seems to assume that bishops, for instance, have arrived. When he speaks of the apostolic orders being akin, in their perfection, to the episcopal state, it means that what he says about apostolic activity is to be understood in the light of this *perfection that has been acquired*. But in the order of a perfection that is still *in fieri*, action will have a somewhat different place. It will be more in the background, simply because the subject who is striving for perfection has not yet reached a degree of contemplation that is capable of overflowing and imparting light and warmth to others.

One very important practical consequence follows from this: that in the business of *acquiring* perfection the life that is led, concretely, in our day and in our country, by the apostolic orders, may not always be quite as propitious as the life led in a contemplative monastery. Assume that one has not yet arrived at the

---

[37] . . . mancando questa (la contemplazione) il carmelitano non puo e non deve essere apostolo. Fr. Anastasio de S. Rosario, O.C.D., "L'eremetismo della regola carmelitana." *Ephemerides Carmeliticae*, Ann. II, Fasc. 1, Feb. 1948.

[38] Pp. 110 ff. N.Y. ed., 1930.

contemplation whose fruits are to be shared with others: is it not possible that the silence of a Cistercian cloister, hidden in the depths of the country, the life of labor, vigils, fasting, penance and constant prayer, may prove to be a more favorable atmosphere for doing so than a college campus in a busy modern city?

Jacques Maritain advances this argument to explain why Pius XI's *Umbratilem* is in no way opposed to St. Thomas's teaching on the superiority of the apostolic life. But this is not the place to quarrel about the merits of religious orders in detail. Each one has its proper place in the Church, each one its dignity, and there can be no question that in the abstract the preaching orders have, and will always retain, the rank of highest dignity. But if they do so, it is above all because they are *de jure* our greatest contemplatives.

Christ Suffers Again

Merton's final periodical piece in this phase of his writing career appeared in *Action Now!* 5, no. 5 (March 1952), 13. It was evidently not written directly for this journal, which was published in St. Louis by the Central Office of the Sodality of Our Lady between 1947 and 1956, but was obtained through the Washington-based Paulist Information Service (mentioned at the conclusion of the piece), a subscription-based source of news and feature articles for a variety of Catholic publications. Brief as it is, the essay is of particular interest because it looks outward on the world beyond the monastery walls, a world of massive violence and injustice, of starvation and mass murder and "the cosmic inhumanity of atomic war"—perhaps the earliest public mention of what would become a decade later a major focus of Merton's attention. In all this Merton sees the ongoing crucifixion of Christ in his members, his Mystical Body, and poses the simple, stark alternative responses to such a state of sinful division—the response of hatred that accepts and increases separation and alienation, that looks to eliminate division by annihilating those from whom we are divided—or the response of love that finds in the crucified and risen Lord the source of healing and of unity, that is willing to suffer together with Christ and with all those least ones, the poor and victimized and abused, with whom Christ has especially identified himself, in order to witness to and participate in the redemptive love that brings persons together with one another and with their Creator. In this brief meditation on the meaning of the cross, this reminder that Christianity is "not merely a doctrine or a system of beliefs" but living in and with Christ and being the presence of Christ in the concrete circumstances of the contemporary world, can be found the seeds of that prophetic witness that would bear much fruit in the final decade of Merton's life.

All over the face of the earth the avarice and lust of men breed unceasing divisions among them, and the wounds that tear men from union with one another widen and open out into huge wars.

Murder, massacres, revolution, hatred, the slaughter and torture of the bodies and souls of men, the destruction of cities by fire, the starvation of millions, the annihilation of populations and finally the cosmic inhumanity of atomic war: Christ is massacred in His members, torn limb from limb; God is murdered in men.

Souls Divided

His physical Body was crucified by Pilate and the Pharisees: His mystical Body is drawn and quartered from age to age by the devils in the agony of that disunion which is bred and vegetates in our souls prone to selfishness and to sin.

The history of the world, with the material destruction of cities and nations and people expresses the division that tyrannizes the souls of all men.

Even the innocent, even those in whom Christ lives by charity, even those who want with their whole heart to love one another, remain divided and separate.

Peace by Annihilation

There are two things which men can do about their pain of disunion with other men. They can love and they can hate.

Hatred recoils from the sacrifice and the sorrow that are the price of the resetting of the broken bones of harmony. It refuses the pain of reunion. It identifies the agony with the other men whose presence causes agony in us by reminding us of our disunion.

Hatred tries to cure disunion by annihilating those who are not united with us. It seeks peace by elimination of everybody else but ourselves.

Christ Unites Men

But love, by its acceptance of the pain of reunion, begins to heal all wounds. It is principally in the suffering and sacrifice that are demanded for men to live together in peace and harmony that love is perfected in us.

For Christianity is not merely a doctrine or a system of beliefs: it is Christ living in us and uniting men to one another in His own Life and unity. "I in them and Thou, Father, in Me, that they may be made perfect in One. . . . And the glory which Thou hast given Me I have given them, that they be one as We also are One."

"He that loveth not abideth in death."

Appendix 1
Textual Notes

ℨ

Poetry and the Contemplative Life

Readings adopted from *Commonweal* text:

10	which somewhat resembles] which sometimes resembles
12	for His action.] for his action.
13	"unitive" or "connatural"] "unitive" of "connatural"

Readings adopted from *Figures for an Apocalypse* text:

5	And yet on] And yet, on
	not all those] not all of those
6	Gregory the Great, and] Gregory the Great and
	faith, in revelation,] faith, by revelation,
7	and the supernatural] and supernatural
	ever even heard] even heard
8	shrink from penance] shrink from facts and penance
9	Bonaventure, Bernard and] Bonaventure, and
10	immediate affective contact] immediate, affective contact
15	from inside the palace] from the inside of the palace
	appall someone] appeal to someone
	end at death . . . our bodies.] end at death.
16	Saint Bonaventure adds] Saint Bonaventure therefore adds

✠   ✠   ✠

Active and Contemplative Orders /
[*The Seven Storey Mountain*, 414–19]

29	have regarded the relation between the active] have looked at the active
30–31	You would have . . . garbled form.] *om.*
31	Not so many . . . eighty-two.] *om.*
	There Saint Thomas comes out] But Saint Thomas also comes out
32	When you see . . . or Saint Bernard:] *om.*
	first comes] First comes
33	men (Serm. 90 de Diversis).] men.
	souls which] souls, which
	Unfortunately . . . itself, the bare] Unfortunately St. Thomas's bare
	turn back the pages to] keep our eyes on
	life of these mixed Orders] "mixed life"
34	contemplative life in Question one eighty-two.] contemplative.
	Therefore it will . . . and no fruits?] *om.*
	the author of this article has no way of] I have no intention of
35	it is at least not] it is not
	We have seen] I just quoted
	came forth] comes out
	elms had taught the Abbot of Clairvaux all his wisdom.] elms taught the monks wisdom.
36	and, indeed, a deep interior life.] and a deep interior life at that.
	If we turn to the pages of] Look in
	what is perhaps the best description ever written] one of the best descriptions ever written
37	example" (Itin, vii. 3).] *example."*
	the very height] the height
	the Seraphic Doctor] St. Bonaventure
	privileged souls, but] privileged monks, but
	Thus all men are called] So any man may be called at least *de jure*, if not *de facto*,
	out of it, no matter] out of it, married or single, no matter

be a contemplative] a deep interior life perhaps even to
mystical prayer,

38   *greater profit to the Church,*] greater profit to the Church,
together" (Spiritual Canticle, b, xxix, 2).] together."
There are degrees . . . Christ's love.] *om.*

Readings adopted from *The Seven Storey Mountain* text:

31   *activa* (the] *activa* the
life). What] life. What

☥   ☥   ☥

Self-Denial and the Christian / Christian Self-Denial
(*Seasons of Celebration* 125–43)

62   **Self-Denial and the Christian] Christian Self-Denial**
demanded that . . . leave] commanded His disciples to
leave

God because . . . their souls.] God. That is to say that
although they might have conceptual knowledge *about*
God and might indeed place Him at the center of their
cosmic outlook and pay Him the respect of their worship,
their life was such that it could in fact dispense with the
"living and efficacious" intervention of His word. In fact
their religion, their philosophy—or else their absence of
either—was not a confession of dependence on God, still
less a way of obedience to His commands, but a way of
existence that justified itself by its implicit belief in man
without God. This way of existence is the "way of the
flesh," that is to say the way of obedience to the "will of
the flesh" or man's will to self-assertion apart from God.
An asceticism that fits into this context of "flesh" may
indeed by [*sic*] very rigorous, extremely "spiritual."
What marks it as "flesh" is its sustained appetite for a
definitively self-achieved "perfection," independently of
our condition of creaturehood.

receiving into . . . Spirit] receiving His word and His
Holy Spirit

(John 8:15) and He added "it] (John 8:15), and He added: "it

On the other hand, those] It is the Spirit of Truth that is
opposed to the "will of the flesh." And here we must try
to distinguish the Biblical concept of man from the
Platonic view which has become almost inseparable
from it in Western thought. The Bible does not divide
man into a spiritual essence (soul) and an accidental
body made of existence and neither of course does
Orthodox Christian theology. Yet in the tradition of
Christian Platonism, magnificent though it may be,
Biblical anthropology has tended to take on a Greek
coloring. The true life of man is said to be the life of the
soul as *distinct from and opposed to* the life of the body.
Christian asceticism comes to be seen as the liberation of
the soul from a kind of "imprisonment" in the body.
Temporal things, belonging to the realm of the body,
are either evil or at best inferior to the spiritual things in
the realm of the soul and of eternity. The "spiritual life"
of man is then a withdrawal from time into eternity, and
this in turn implies neglect of or contempt for the ordinary temporal active life of everyday. "Spirituality" then
seems to demand the negation of everyday reality and a
withdrawal into a realm of angels and pure essences,
where eventually "union with God" will be attained
outside time and beyond the contamination of all that is
bodily and temporal.

Is this a genuinely Christian perspective? Is the function of self-denial merely to "liberate the soul" and
withdraw it from temporal distractions and cares? Is not
Christianity rather a humble and realistic acceptance of
everyday life and of God's will in a spirit of obedience
and liberty? Is not the true function of our self-denial the
clarification of God's will in our regard, and the *unification*
of our whole being, body and soul, in His service?

Those

by this same Spirit,] by His Spirit,

their souls. And] their entire being and manifests itself in
all their activities, body and soul. The

false values of the world, and] false ego-centered values
and

flesh, to live] flesh (i.e., the ego-centered self), to live

63   entitled. It . . . even] entitled. Even
         those who say they believe] those who believe
         good things of the present life.] affirmation of the "flesh"
           in ego-centered satisfactions.
         meat and . . . profit. Nevertheless,] meat. Nevertheless,
         great Carmelite] Spanish Carmelite
64   St. Thomas . . . in our souls.] However, though it may
           be quite true that the genuine happiness of the human
           person is only attained when the self breaks out of its
           own narrow limits and is delivered from fixation upon
           its own satisfaction and affirmation, this is not the reason
           for Christian self-denial. There can be a genuine Christian
           Eudaimonism, or philosophy of happiness, and there is
           certainly such a thing as Christian humanism. An apolo-
           getic appeal to these values may be legitimate and may
           perhaps help to defend the Church against the accusation
           of remaining bogged down in Medievalism (as if there
           had been no happiness in the Middle Ages!). However,
           even if self-denial did not bring with it a certain satisfac-
           tion and an enlargement of our human capacities,
           it would still be necessary, because without it the
           Christian life cannot be fully centered on the essential
           obedience we owe to God, not only as our Creator but
           also as our Redeemer.
               The call to "do penance" is based not on the fact that
           penance will keep us in trim, but on the fact that
           "the Kingdom of Heaven is at hand." Our penance—
           metanoia—is our response to the proclamation of the
           Gospel message, the *Kerygma* which announces our
           salvation if we will hear God and not harden our hearts.
           The function of penance and self-denial is then *contrition,*
           or the "breaking up" of that hardness of heart which
           prevents us from understanding God's command to
           love, and from obeying it effectively.
         to do so we] to do this we
         with the life of grace.] with the law of love and of grace.
         the Christian program of asceticism] the Christian
           asceticism
         life. It is the source . . . the trellis] life. It is the trellis

65   complete manual of] complete source of
than the Missal.] than the Liturgy.
Epistles and Gospels,] Psalms and Bible texts,
offer, by reading . . . of abnegation.] offer by active and
  intelligent participation is the normal expression of
  Christian metanoia.
flatter human nature by] flatter the ego by
with the hope . . . here and now.] to understand that our
  existence in "the world" and in time becomes fruitful
  and meaningful in proportion as we are able to assume
  spiritual and Christian responsibility for our life, our
  work, and even for the world we live in. Thus Christian
  asceticism does not provide a flight from the world,
  a refuge from the stress and distraction of manifold
  wickedness. It enables us to enter into the confusion of
  the world bearing something of the light of Truth in our
  hearts, and capable of exercising something of the
  mysterious, transforming power of the Cross, of love
  and of sacrifice.

    But in that case, self-denial must mean something
  more than the triumph of our good self over our evil self,
  of reason over compulsion, or even more naively, of
  "soul" over "body." Actually it is not a question of
  resolving a conflict between two forces in ourselves but
  of submitting our whole being to the will of God in the
  "obedience of faith." This means much more than simply
  doing good and avoiding evil, much more than simply
  acquiring inner peace, and certainly more than just
  becoming thoroughly respectable and pious. It means
  entering into the Paschal Mystery of the death and
  resurrection of Christ by the total conversion of our
  entire self to Him by the Cross and a new life.
What is the Mass? It is a] Liturgy is a
are already beginning . . . on earth.] are building the
  Kingdom of Heaven on earth and in history.

66   profound and sweet] profound, sweet
the priest has received and distributed Communion.]
  people of God have received the Body and Blood of the
  Risen Savior:

for our sanctification] for our conversion and
   sanctification
in our souls? He] in our lives? He
souls and bodies] souls, bodies
into Himself.] in His will.
can find . . . can finally] can finally appreciate
be a blessing.] be "the liberty of the sons of God."
67   transformation in Christ.] transformation in Christ. He is
   the one who makes our life and work in the world a
   sterile and trivial assertion of our own futility.
fight creatures] control our natural love for good things
as she frequently does,] as she does,
the inordinate . . . is evil.] an ego-centered love of the
   good things of life is a source of darkness and evil in the
   world.
of Holy Saturday, at] the Paschal Vigil at
68   be absolutely rooted] be rooted
the Christian soul.] the Christian life. Self-denial is then
   directed to this process of uprooting and liberation.
using creatures] using the goods of life
and use and desire] and use and love
every field and farm.] every field.
own soul, and he] own being. He
69   order was turned] order has been turned
by original sin.] by sin.
The soul that is outside] The man who is outside
this sad state.] this state.
the merits of Calvary] the power of Calvary
be applied to a soul] avail in a life
belong to creatures.] belong to our own ego.
The real function . . . to shame.] The real purpose of
   Christian asceticism is then not to liberate the soul from
   the desires and needs of the body, but to bring the whole
   man into complete submission to God's will as expressed
   in the concrete demands of life in all its existential reality.
   A spirituality that merely entrenched a man in the
   privacy of his own will and his own ego beyond the
   reach of all the claims of flesh, of history and of time,
   would not only be futile, but it might also confirm him

in the evil of that spurious autonomy which is deaf to
the call to salvation and obedience uttered in the Gospel
Kerygma.

Self-denial is useless unless it opens the ears of our
heart to obey the will of God commanding us to take our
place in time, in history and in the work of building His
Kingdom of Love and Truth. An asceticism that fails in
this may actually strengthen our opposition and resistance to God by making us concentrate on our own
autonomy and moral perfection instead of on the concrete obligation to love God and our fellow man.

the Christian soul as an] the Christian as an
deadening of natural vitality.] control of instinct by
    deadening the appetites of the heart.
70 our soul, to the exact] our whole being to the exact
Father. Neglect . . . of the soul.] Father
nature. It does . . . soul. It frustrates] nature. It frustrates
destroy it. But it] destroy it. But this
depths of the soul,] "depths of the soul,"
dispositions of soul.] dispositions.
crude and human way] crude and inhuman way
proud and irritable and uncharitable.] proud, irritable and
    gross.
fanatics and have persecuted the saints and] fanatics, have
    persecuted the saints, and
The function of self-denial is to bring] Self-denial can
    assuredly bring
cares and worries and sorrows] cares, worries, sorrows
Asceticism is . . . it roots] Asceticism roots
71 ten children to look after as] ten children as
monk. In] monk—or vice versa! In
mother.] mother.

However, we must not imagine that the way of self-
denial is always a way of tranquility and uninterrupted
peace. It does not resolve all doubts and deliver us from
every care as if by magic. Self-denial attunes us to the
Spirit of God and the Spirit may not always sing a tune
that harmonizes with our nature. There may be terrible
discords instead of tranquil harmonies. Self-denial

brings order into our lives sometimes in the form of an apparent disorder, and we may sometimes have to find peace as best we can in the midst of confusion. What matters is not the tranquility of our own heart but the sincerity of our faith and the totality of our obedience to God. But before we can begin to obey Him we must first recognize how profoundly inclined we are to disobey, and how difficult it really is for us to embrace a way of obedience to grace that means letting go of the security of our own self-hood and our own nature.

That is why the desire for ascetic works that pacify our minds and give us a sense of achievement may in fact prove to be an escape from the true and radical self-denial required of us by God.

direction) all] direction), all
work and rests] work, rests
the Blessed Trinity in the depths of his soul.] the indwelling Spirit.
obligation. That is a good sign. Wherever] obligation. Wherever

71–72   flesh." He lets . . . around them. Pleasures] flesh." Pleasures

72   these generous souls to do] these Christians to do
But the more . . . all in all.] At the same time they become deeply aware of the radical insufficiency of arbitrarily chosen "ascetic practices" and of "methods" which are simply aimed at resolving moral conflicts within the self and establishing the ego in a peaceful equilibrium.
The true self-denial of the Christian is not a conquest of himself by himself, but a dying to self in order to live to God in Christ. This is the great question that preoccupied St. Paul—the problem of seeking salvation by the works of the law instead of by grace. Our salvation is not to be found in asceticism alone but in the Cross of Christ. Self-denial, however rigorous, lacks all Christian meaning apart from the Cross and Resurrection of Christ.

This is why Lent is a season of mortification and renouncement: not just because Christians discovered that a little fasting in Springtime was good for their constitutions, but because their fasts, renunciations and alms deeds had an essential part to play as signs of a full participation in the Easter Mystery.

The Church has relaxed the general laws of fasting in Lent, but this does not mean that Lent has now ceased to be a season of fasting and self-denial. It remains for the individual Christian, in the sincerity of his own conscience before God, to undertake such acts of self-denial and charity as will truly signify his will to die to himself and live in the Spirit of the Risen Christ.

Appendix 2

States of Life

John Fearon, O.P.

The religious orders have always been a significant factor in the life of the Church, contributing either to her embarrassment by their failures or to her triumph by their successes. Accordingly, a correct evaluation of the religious state in general and an adequate appraisal of the various types into which that state is divided are of the utmost importance to all interested in the triumph of the Church. It is to be regretted that by an unfortunate paradox in the history of Christian spirituality modern thought on the religious state, instead of being clearer and better developed than ancient thought, is actually more confused. The varieties of the religious state and their relationships to the development of Christian perfection and the good of the Church have been subjected by modern authors to confusion and distortion, whereas in the minds of the great doctors of the past all was clear and orderly. An example of this unhappy contrast may be found in the remarkable lucidity of one of these great doctors of the past, St. Thomas Aquinas, and the distressing confusion of one of these modern authors, the Trappist poet, Thomas Merton. They are definitely at odds in the important matter of the relative merits and the difference of function of the active and contemplative orders.

146

Inasmuch as modern works on Christian morality often lack a properly theological consideration of the special states of the Christian life and the ordinary theological course today treats of the religious life in a cursory and inadequate fashion, it seems well to present the doctrine of St. Thomas on the active and contemplative lives, and on the religious state and its formal variants. Following this exposition we shall contrast the teaching of the Angelic Doctor with the modern viewpoint referred to above.[1] In conclusion, we shall attempt to indicate a few of the many practical conclusions, important to everyone, which issue from St. Thomas' treatment of the religious life.

I

In ordinary speech, the terms "life" and "state" can have reference to such things as magazines and civil institutions, yet a misunderstanding of the usage of these terms is unlikely. In ordinary speech, however, such terms as "contemplative life" and "contemplative order," "religious life" and "religious order," or "religious state," are frequently confused. Not so in theology. Theologically, the contemplative religious state and the active religious state are defined and differentiated in terms of the works of the active and contemplative lives, but neither *state* is to be confused with its corresponding type of *life*. In much the same fashion, the medical profession and the culinary profession are defined and differentiated in terms of the works of the sciences of medicine and cooking, in terms of health and nutrition, and yet they are not identified with health and nutrition. Fruitful theological thought on this subject must keep this distinction clearly in mind. An understanding of the relative merits of the contemplative and active lives must include some idea of the thing divided, an insight into the type of distinction involved, and knowledge of the standards according to which the judgment is to be made.

---

[1] Cf. T. Merton, "Active and Contemplative Orders," *The Commonweal*, XLVII, No. 8.

"Life," as divided into "contemplative" and "active," is not simply self-motion, a feature common to all living things. The distinction between the contemplative and the active life applies specifically to human life, intelligent and rational life. In this sense we are accustomed to say that a man leads the life of a philosopher or the life of a sportsman inasmuch as his greatest delight and chief interest is either in thought or in athletic accomplishments. Accordingly, "life" as divided into "contemplative" and "active" refers to the rational and deliberate side of human life. And a form of life in this sense is denominated as active or contemplative by what is chiefly intended in that life. Inasmuch as some men chiefly intend the contemplation of truth and others chiefly intend an exterior type of activity, human life can be conveniently divided into active and contemplative.

This distinction is adequate and sufficient. The thing divided is the intellectual life of man, that type of self-motion which is his alone, not the vegetative and sensitive life he has in common with his pets. That intellectual life and its resultant knowledge, from the view point of goal or end, is either an end in itself or a means to action, speculative or practical. It is precisely from this point of view that human life is divided into contemplative and active. In the abstract, this distinction is obviously sufficient. In the concrete, however, no man's life is entirely one or the other; every man's life must be a combination of both. Even the metaphysician has to know how to tie his shoes. Yet even in the concrete a man's principal intention cannot be equally centered on both lives. Hence even in the concrete the distinction is sufficient. A shoe-tying metaphysician is still principally a metaphysician. Evaluating these two lives and assigning a position of priority to one or the other, may be accomplished with accuracy only upon the basis of a threefold consideration of priority: a priority of nature, a priority of merit, and a priority in the order of generation.

From the viewpoint of the nature of the thing involved, i.e. human life, that life will be superior in which the conditions of human felicity are more fully realized. St. Thomas gives eight reasons for the primacy of the contemplative life. First, the contemplative life is an exercise of the noblest faculty of man, the intellect, and it considers the noblest object of that faculty, intelligible being, principally God. Secondly, the contemplative life is more continuous. Thirdly, the contemplative life is more delightful. Fourthly, in the contemplative life a man is more self-sufficient since he needs less. Fifthly, because it is more true of the contemplative life that it is desirable simply for itself and not as a means to something else, it is more perfect than the active. Sixthly, the contemplative life is more quiet. Seventhly, the contemplative life is more closely associated with divine life, whereas the active life is more closely associated with human life. Finally, the contemplative life is more purely intellectual than the active life, which involves the operation of other human faculties.

From the viewpoint of merit St. Thomas holds that in itself the contemplative life is more meritorious than the active. He argues to this position from the following premises: charity is the root of merit; charity consists in the love of God and neighbor and is more meritorious in those acts which directly pertain to the love of God than in those which directly pertain to the love of neighbor; the contemplative life is directly concerned with directly loving God whereas the active life is directly concerned with directly loving neighbor. It can and does happen however, that because of the charity of the one meriting a work of the active life is more meritorious when done with greater charity than a work of the contemplative life done with lesser charity. This consideration in no way militates against St. Thomas' objective conclusion; it is merely a question of which visitor gets the best bed in the house, the prince or the pauper. The answer is simple except in the case where the pauper happens to have a special claim on one's affections. Finally, in the order of generation the situation of primacy is reversed. As embraced by men, the active life is a disposition for the exercise of contemplation. Unquiet human nature must first be brought under control before contemplation is a possibility to any great extent.

The various religious states are defined, differentiated, and evaluated in terms of the works of the active and contemplative lives. Yet the terms "contemplative religious state" and "contemplative life," "active religious state" and "active life" are not to be confused. St. Thomas treats of life and state in two distinct sections. However, it is true that an antecedent understanding of the two lives and their relative merits is essential to an understanding of his thought on the various religious states and their relative merits. In general, the religious state is defined by St. Thomas as a state of perfection. Accordingly, before approaching the question of the varieties of religious state and their relative merits, an appreciation of the terms state and perfection is indispensable.

In abstract terms, "state" properly signifies an immovable condition of a thing disposed in a way suitable to its nature. Etymologically the term comes from the word "stand," in which position the natural disposition of one's members is verified, *sc.*, head up and feet on the ground, though indeed in a movable way. However, in human affairs the term "state" has been transferred to signify an immovable condition in factors which are internal, invariable, and personal. Theologically it does not refer to such external variable factors as wealth or poverty. The element of immobility in that condition is verified by a permanence of personal obligation. Thus, in this restricted sense, state is properly predicated only of freedom or servitude whether in spiritual or civil affairs.

State is thus immediately subdivided into the state of freedom and the state of servility. In the spiritual order, each of these states is subdivided into that of beginner, proficient, and perfect with respect either to good or evil, the true state of freedom being one of virtue, the true state of servitude being one of vice. Yet it is to be noted that whereas the states of slavery and freedom are specifically different, the states of beginner, proficient, and perfect differ by way of emphasis.

Human perfection essentially consists in charity. Yet charity is a virtue capable of growth. The outstanding steps in this growth have been isolated by the doctors of the Church on the basis of difference in emphasis. Thus they distinguish a state of beginners in which emphasis must be placed on the avoiding of sin and the resistance of evil inclinations. In the second stage, that of proficients, emphasis is on the very process of increasing in charity itself. Finally, they distinguish a third stage, that of the perfect, in which primacy of interest is simply that they cling to God and enjoy union with Him. When St. Thomas refers to the religious state as a state of perfection he means perfection in this latter sense. Just as the commandments impose obligations which remove those things contrary to charity in the absolute sense, so too the counsels are ordained to removing impediments to the development of charity into the third stage, *sc.*, that of the perfect. Yet the impediments to the presence of charity in the human will are things in themselves evil, whereas the impediments to the growth of charity are not, e.g., matrimony, worldly business, and the like. Hence the religious state consists essentially in the assumption of the counsels as obligations. Since state is an immovable condition this obligation must be permanent and solemn, i.e., one of public vow recognized as such by the Church. For this reason the religious state is in a special sense a state of perfection.

Thus, paradoxically, a man perfect in charity in the sense that his prime interest is union with God, although he is not solemnly bound by vows to the obligation of following the counsels, is not in the state of perfection. And a religious bound by vow to the obligation of following the counsels yet chiefly interested in avoiding sin is in the state of perfection. For though man's spiritual condition before God is of greater importance than obligations recognized in and by the Church, it is this solemn obligation and not simply charity that places him in a state of perfection, as that term is used by St. Thomas.

The question now arises as to whether there is such a thing as variety in religious institutes and if so is it possible to grade them in an order of excellence. In the first place, a religious institute as an exemplification of the religious state is a school in which men are habituated or trained in the perfection of charity. And inasmuch as there are diverse works of charity and diverse methods of training, it is possible to ascertain differences in religious orders. On the one hand, they can be distinguished by their goals, that is by the diversity of works to which various institutes are ordered, as, e.g., the care of the sick, or the redemption of captives. On the other hand, they can be distinguished by the diversity of practice, e.g., some castigate the body by fasting, some by manual labor, and some by standing in cold water. Since goals are universally significant and, relative to societies, are in fact specificative, the prime differences in religious institutes must be considered from the view point of goal. Indeed it is true that there is a certain community of goal or intention in all religious institutes and a certain community of practice, *sc.*, the vows. Yet both goals and methods admit of an element of variation which constitutes true differences. This variety has been always introduced and conserved by the authority of the Holy See as of maximum importance for the good of the Church as a whole.

St. Thomas holds that the varieties of the religious state are not only defined and differentiated but also evaluated in terms of the active and contemplative lives. And in an orderly fashion he lays down the standards according to which that judgment is to be made. Differences on the part of goal are more important than differences on the part of method. Things can be contrasted only in those aspects in which they differ, hence the relative excellence of a religious institute flows from differences with respect to goals primarily and to method secondarily. The comparison from the part of goal is absolute inasmuch as goals are sought for themselves; comparison on the part of method is relative, for methods are good only in terms of their efficiency in obtaining the goal.

The works of the active life to which a religious institute may be ordered as to a goal are twofold: some by their very nature are derived from the fullness of contemplation—teaching and preaching sacred doctrine; others, such as giving alms and caring for the sick, are totally exterior occupations and are not of their very nature derived from the fullness of contemplation. The first type of work is preferable to simple contemplation by way of addition for it is better to illumine than merely to shine. Both the first type of work of the active life and simple contemplation are preferable to the second type of work of the active life. The validity of this evaluation of works has already been established in the consideration of the active and contemplative lives. Accordingly, from the viewpoint of goal, orders which are ordained to preaching and teaching rank first, those which are ordered simply to contemplation rank second, and those which are occupied with exterior works of the active life of the second type rank third. Within each of these three classifications preëminence of various institutes is to be estimated: first, by more detailed gradations of the work involved; secondly, by the number of works which can possibly multiply excellence; and thirdly, by the proportionate effectiveness of the statutes of each institute to accomplish proposed goals. In this evaluation St. Thomas is speaking of instances of the religious state and not of individual religious and their particular degree of holiness. All the religious orders have this in common, that they tend toward the perfection of charity. It would be a distortion of the text of St. Thomas to say that simply active orders tend only toward the initial stage of perfection. Also, it is to be noted that it is not the multitude or intensity of exercises that establishes the relative excellence of method but their proportion to the goal, their effectiveness in attaining the end of the order. This is not a concrete evaluation of religious orders based upon the spirituality of their actual members, but an objective analysis of the nature of these institutes as stipulated in their statutes. This is a brief summary of the mind of St. Thomas on the active and contemplative lives, and on the religious state and its varieties. It has been culled from his tract on the different lives[2] and from his tract on the different states.[3]

II

The task of criticising Thomas Merton's article[4] is made difficult by the fact that his sequence of thought is somewhat perplexing. Lest this criticism suffer that same disadvantage, we will offer: first, a general criticism of the argument as a whole; secondly, a particular criticism of particular parts. The author of this article proposes as his object the "argument 'action vs. contemplation' . . . ." Specifically he attempts "to reconcile" an alleged contrariety between St. Thomas' teaching[5] that the "mixed vocation" is superior to the contemplative or active vocation and his doctrine[6]

---

[2] *Summa Theol.*, II–II, qq. 179–182.
[3] *Ibid.*, qq. 183–189.
[4] *Loc. cit.*
[5] *Summa Theol.*, II–II, q. 188, a. 6.
[6] *Ibid.*, q. 182, a. 1.

that the contemplative life in itself by its very nature is superior to the active life. This proposed reconciliation is effected by a reference to qualifications of the general doctrine by St. Thomas himself and by an interpretation of what St. Thomas must have meant in the light of traditional teaching.

As regards the first article of the one hundred eighty-second question, the author insists that the general evaluation of the two lives must be qualified by the doctrine contained in the response to the third objection to that article. "When he admits that the active life *can* be more perfect under certain circumstances, accidentally, he hedges his statement with half a dozen qualifications of a strictness that greatly enhances what he has already said about contemplation. First, activity will only be more perfect than the joy and rest of contemplation if it is undertaken as the result of an overflow of love for God . . . in order to fulfil His will. It is not to be continuous, only the answer to a temporary emergency. It is purely for God's glory, and it does not dispense us from contemplation. It is an added obligation, and we must return as soon as we morally can to the powerful and fruitful silence of recollection that disposes our souls for divine union."[7]

In view of this response and in view of traditional teaching, the author offers his interpretation of the sixth article, question one hundred eighty-eight, which evaluates the various types of religious orders. By active orders he says that St. Thomas here "clearly" means orders engaged in external works of charity or mercy for the good of others. He says that the bare statement "the religious institutes which are ordered to the work of preaching and teaching hold the highest rank in religion" is frankly misleading and conjures up nothing more than a mental image of some pious and industrious clerics bustling from the library to the classroom. Finally, he maintains that in ranking the three types of institute St. Thomas was obviously thinking of the traditional conception of the degrees of perfection so explicitly found in St. Augustine and St. Bernard. Accordingly, as he sees it, by the

---

[7] Merton, *loc. cit.*

"mixed" orders St. Thomas must really have meant the peak of the mystical life, the marriage of the soul to God, which gives the saints a miraculous power and smooth and tireless energy in working for God and souls.

By arguing that all religious, and in fact all lay people, do (or at least should) in some sense arrive at this peak of mystical life, the author considers that he has reconciled the contrariety between the two texts of St. Thomas and has exposed the true meaning of the Angelic Doctor. By way of corollary he concludes that all orders are best, that there is only one vocation for all since all are called to the summit of perfection, and that degrees and varieties in perfection, i.e., of religious vocations, depend on the perfection of divine union and not on the means the order has at its disposal for preaching and teaching.

In the first place, it is necessary to say that there is no such contrariety as the author alleges between the two texts cited from the *Summa*, nor is there any need for a reconciliation of them. Only on the basis of an inexcusable confusion between St. Thomas' concepts of life and state could such a contrariety be envisaged. The exception cited from the response to the third objection of the first article, question one hundred eighty-two, is not an exception to the superiority of the contemplative life over the active life. The response merely states that in certain circumstances the *works* of the active life can be superior to the *works* of the contemplative life. It makes no specific reference to types of active work done, e.g., preaching, or caring for the sick. The assumption of such works according to the stated circumstances would in no way vary the species of the contemplative life which is established by primacy of intention.

In the sixth article, question one hundred eighty-eight, St. Thomas treats of the varieties and grades of the religious state. Inasmuch as the religious state is a state of perfection, all varieties and grades of that state have as a common intention and goal perfection, in the sense of perfection in charity, without relation to the initial and proficient grades of charity. It is common to all religious institutes that they pertain to the religious *state*, and constitution in this state depends, not upon simple intention, but upon the formal assumption of the counsels as personal obligations. St. Thomas was not assuming the grades of charity of St. Augustine and St. Bernard as the basis for his differentiation and gradation of religious institutes. Actually he is both clear and explicit as to his foundation for differentiation and gradation, *sc.*, the goals of the various institutes considered in terms of the active and contemplative lives. He indicates two types of work of the active life: some which of their nature flow from the abundance of contemplation—preaching and teaching, and others which of their nature do not, i.e., the giving of alms and the reception of travelers. Seen in this light, St. Thomas' conception of the most perfect type of religious institute suggests something far superior to the image of pious and industrious clerics bustling from the library to the classroom, which Thomas Merton seems to have drawn from it.

The author appears to conclude too widely in judging that all orders and all Christians do or should live according to a pattern which mixes the works of the contemplative and active life,[8] and thus fulfill the vocation of the most perfect type of religious institute as described by St. Thomas.[9] For St. Thomas, to contemplate and to pass on to others the fruit of contemplation has a very specific meaning. Some works of their very nature are fruits of contemplation, *sc.*, preaching and teaching sacred doctrine. Praying for others and being an example of contemplative perfection are not works of the active life which of their nature flow from the abundance of contemplation. They are part and parcel of the contemplative life in the sense of being solely contemplative. Indeed the abbot might strictly give to the community the fruits of his contemplation; but he is only the abbot, he is not the institute; his role is not the specific goal of the institute. The Little Sister of the Poor who has an intense interior life and cares for the aged is not giving of the fruits of contemplation in the strict sense. Such religious are doing works of the purely active life and are merely being good religious in the process. A religious of the most perfect

[8] Cf. *Summa Theol.*, II–II, q. 182, a. 1, ad Sum.
[9] *Ibid.*, q. 188, a. 6.

type of religious institute should engage in the works of the active life, *sc.*, preaching and teaching in conformity with the conditions laid down by St. Thomas.[10] It does not logically follow that every type of activity (e.g., caring for the sick, redeeming captives, being an example of contemplative perfection, praying for others) is a giving to others the fruits of contemplation. Strictly speaking, these works are not the fruits of contemplation. Hence it is absolutely false to conclude that there is only one type of religious state and one vocation.

The author's corollaries as well, seem to be at variance with the doctrine of St. Thomas. Degrees and varieties of religious vocation (i.e., vocation in the objective sense of *state*) do most certainly depend upon the works to which the various institutes are ordained, e.g., preaching, teaching, etc. In St. Thomas, the degree of union with God has nothing to do with this problem. The author has completely obliterated all bases for differences in religious institutes and has also overemphasized their common element, *sc.*, their tendency to the perfection of charity, but this is not the thought of St. Thomas.

Moreover, the author's division of religious institutes into contemplative, active, and mixed is not an exact rendering of St. Thomas' doctrine. These "mixed" orders in St. Thomas are orders whose goal is works of the active life which of their nature flow from the abundance of contemplation, not just any works of the active life. The simple term "mixed" in no way conveys this exactitude of thought. The author is also of the opinion that St. Thomas uses the term "active life" in two different ways, i.e., to denote (1) external acts of charity and mercy for the good of others; (2) as the activity required for the practice of any virtue by anyone in the purgative or illuminative ways. He thinks the Doctor changes from one sense to the other without giving any warning when he is about to make the change. It is true that St. Thomas uses the term "active life" in slightly varying senses, but the

[10] *Ibid.*, q. 182, a. 1, ad 5um.

opinion that this change in sense occurs in a confusing manner is without foundation.

In the opinion of the Trappist author, the "mixed" orders today in America realize their vocation to contemplate and give to others the fruit of their contemplation by way of compromise, *sc.*, by dividing their duties between their nuns and their priests. The nuns live in cloisters and do the contemplating and the priests live in colleges and cities and do the teaching and preaching. As a matter of fact the goals and statutes of the "mixed" orders in America today are the same as they were since their foundations in Europe. Though they may fail to realize their ideal to a certain degree, a failure that is easily understandable considering the height of the ideal, compromise has not taken place either legally or factually, nor has it even been considered. In the article under consideration the author makes an evaluation of the "mixed" and contemplative orders according to two different standards. He evaluates the "mixed" orders in America today according to what he thinks has actually happened to them, and evaluates the contemplative orders in terms of their statutes. Such a difference of standard might have the advantage of being rhetorically strong, but it has the disadvantage of being logically very weak.

The author attempts to prove that the Carthusians are a mixed order in the most flattering sense of the term because they copy books, that the Cistercians are a mixed order because they once produced a school of mystical theology, and that the nursing sisterhoods are mixed because they have a deep interior life. In this he fails to prove his point. "Mixed" orders are such because they have for their goal works of the active life which of their nature flow from contemplation. Copying books hardly seems to be a work of that nature. It is rather difficult to see how taking a sick man's temperature with a thermometer is an operation of its very nature flowing from the abundance of contemplation. His example of an ecstacy of St. Bonaventure as a typical instance of giving to others the fruit of contemplation is not an example of that fruit at all. An ecstacy is not a work of the active life. If the aim of this article was to convince Christians, both religious and lay, that they subjectively had a vocation to the mystical life, then the argument the author chose was peculiarly inappropriate. The tract in the *Summa*, upon which the conclusions are based can not lead to the author's conclusion, if the tract is properly understood.

III

The evolution of the Church in a given area can be divided into three general stages. Initially, the major burden of the missionary effort is to make the Church visible in that area. The second phase of development consists in establishing the Church on a more or less self-sufficient basis from the view point of finances and clergy. The final and lengthiest stage of that evolution is basically a matter of bringing the members of the Church to the perfection of the Christian life and bringing the population of that territory into the Church. These various stages require diverse abilities and diverse agencies in the forces which are attempting to bring about growth. This generation in America is perhaps the first to see the day when the missionary and second stage of development are more or less completed. Accordingly, the Church in the United States today is at a point when special emphasis needs to be placed on those special abilities and agencies whose peculiar work it is to bring the Church to perfection.

In this historical context one of the first practical applications of St. Thomas' doctrine on the differentiation and gradation of religious institutes is that these institutes whose special work it is to bring the Church to perfection need to be encouraged. For the most part the work of bringing the members of the Church to the perfection of the Christian life is one of preaching and teaching sacred doctrine. On the other hand the great bulk of men outside the Church belong to the rather well-educated but unreligious class we ordinarily characterize as secular. To date no effective apologetic methods have been devised to bring this class of men into the Church. But this much is clear: the work is going to have to be done by men who are thoroughly spiritual, in a word— contemplatives, and by men who are intellectually equipped by specialized doctrinal preparation, by men who actually, personally, have contact with that class. In other words one of the most vital needs of the Church in America today is healthy and numerous institutes of the so-called "mixed" type whose special goal is the work of preaching and teaching, works which of their nature flow from the abundance of contemplation.

Religious institutes of all types generally adapt themselves to the conditions of time and place and adjust themselves to the needs of the Church at the given moment. Thus, for example, it happens that institutes with different goals will all engage in missionary activity in the initial phase of the life of the Church in a given territory. Yet in the final process of bringing the Church to perfection it is of the utmost importance that their particular goals and their specialization of activities be reemphasized. Hence the needs of the American Church in our day call for a general return by religious institutes to the works for which they were originally approved and to which their manner of life is best proportioned.

As a further practical application of the thought of St. Thomas on the varieties of the religious state and the standards whereby the different institutes are to be evaluated, it might be noted that it would be well if those actually engaged in vocational guidance would keep them in mind. Those burdened with the duty of providing vocational advice to youth should be perfectly familiar not only with the different types of work done by each institute but also with the proportion the observances of each institute bear to the intended goal. A valid judgment of a religious institute must be made from both points of view. Vocational guidance should not be a mere process of populating a favorite community or recommending the institute which is most arduous in the sense that its observances are absolutely the most rigorous. In conclusion it might be well to recall that St. Thomas maintains that the differences in religious institutes are for the beauty and good of the Church. Both from the viewpoint of doctrine and from the viewpoint of practical attitudes, questions of difference in kind and difference of degree should be approached with that consideration first and foremost in mind and heart.

College of St. Albert the Great,
Oakland, California.

Entering the Silence 266–70

January 22, 1949. Third Sunday after Epiphany
So I sit down to figure out an article in *The Thomist* which has gone to the great trouble of refuting something I must have said somewhere about contemplation. I am very flattered at being refuted by learned men. It almost makes me feel as if my opinions were important—almost, but not quite.

However, what does he say?

First, I have not clearly distinguished between the contemplative *life* and the contemplative *state*. So, here comes St. Thomas' doctrine first of all: the division of active and contemplative—divides the intellectual life of man into two kinds, depending on what is chiefly intended by that life—contemplation of truth or external activity. This distinction is sufficient in the abstract. In the concrete, every life is a combination. But a man's principal intention will still be centered on one or the other. (This is good—tapped as one of my mistakes in that A.[ctive] C.[ontemplative] article.)

Evaluate them all to three priorities:

A. priority of nature—contemplative life 1st—makes men happier. St. Thomas' eight reasons.

B. priority of merit—contemplative life 1st: *per se* contemplative life directly concerned with charity—root of merit. (*per accidens* active life can be more meritorious.)

C. priority of *generation*—active life (practice of virtues). Now, religious *state* [underlined twice]. He admits that the "states" are dedicated to the works of the active or contemplative "lives" and, therefore, understanding of the two *lives* is essential for understanding states.

State = condition of stability dependent on permanent personal obligation. State of perfection (all religious Orders) primary interest to cling to God and enjoy union with Him; practice counsels to remove impediments to this—assumes counsels as obligations.

(i.e. more or less external and legal definition—a man can be a saint and not be in this "*state* of perfection," i.e., not a religious.

Active state – a) purely active b) derived from *fullness of contemplation*

Contemplative state – c

b & c preferable by virtue of their *works* to a.

So far, O.K. The part about Thomas Merton is cockeyed. He got it all distorted. He thinks I am trying to reshuffle St. Thomas' technical distinctions into different exterior categories when all I am saying is that in *practice* every Christian is called to close union with God and to share with others the fruits of that union one way or another—certainly not all by being teachers!!! God forbid!

However, I suppose I was really pretending to analyze St. Thomas in order to put this across in a way that resulted in misinterpretation.

He winds up by stating what I wanted to state, but in such a way that it loses all its punch: that those engaged in "works flowing from the fullness of contemplation" ought to be contemplatives. He nowhere in the article says what he or St. Thomas means by contemplation. And in effect his conclusion is that the Dominicans, etc., ought to be supplied with good vocations to make sure that they will make an impression on the non-Catholic intelligentsia.

January 24, 1949

This *Thomist* article—points against me:

1. "The sequence of thought is rather perplexing." p.g. *concedo* [I concede].

2. I am supposed to argue "that all religious and all lay people do (or at least should) in some sense arrive at this peak of mystical

life the author (me) considers he has reconciled the contrariety . . ." but g. and 188 a. b. *do—nego prorsus* [I absolutely disagree].

3. He concludes that there is only one vocation—yes, to *perfection*: but not technically one "vocation" in the juridical sense.

4. and that degrees and varieties in perfection of religious vocations depend on *the perfection of divine union and not on the means the Order has at its disposal for teaching and preaching*.

His point of view—which is correct in its own way—is that St. Thomas was not attempting "a concrete evaluation of religious orders based on the spirituality of their actual members, *but on an objective analysis of the nature of these institutes . . .*" That this is St. Thomas' view—*concedo*.

That I was confusing the issue in taking the *concrete, factual* view based on individual sanctity—*concedo*. It made me miss the target, but it does not affect the truth of the statement I was really trying to prove. This is simply that, since the works of the preaching orders are "by their very nature derived from *the fullness of contemplation*," *a certain fullness or perfection of contemplation* is required for the institute to carry out its function. Whether that fullness implies infused contemplation (and hence an obligation of the members of such an institute to lead lives *tending* to infused contemplation) I did not say and neither did Fr. F., but it is important someone should have taken it up. Also, in saying that the dignity of the preaching orders springs not from the *fact* [underlines twice] that they preach, but the fact that preaching is supposed to be derived from the fullness of contemplation. It is thus the *contemplative* element, and not the active element, that gives the works of this life their superior dignity.

However, if he had taken the trouble to wipe his glasses, he would have seen that I was basing my own interpretation of the mixed vocations as taken in the concrete on *St. Bonaventure* who does take it so in the text I quoted. He says the term "mixed" orders is not exact.

5. "*It is absolutely false to conclude that there is only one type of religious and one vocation.*" In the juridical sense, *concedo*. That was not my intention. I was speaking of the general vocation of all Christians to perfect charity and even to the contemplative *life* (not contemplative *state*) in some degree, and perhaps even to share

the fruits of contemplation (but not in the strict, technical sense of preaching and teaching).

6. "Degrees and varieties of religious vocation (i.e., vocation in the objective sense of state) do most certainly depend upon the works to which the various institutions are ordained." *Concedo.* But here is the point I hold on to: works flowing from the fullness of contemplation *ipso facto* imply a certain fullness of contemplation. Even taking vocation in the sense of a juridical state this is true. To be obliged by vow to do works that flow from the fullness of contemplation is to be obliged in some sense to tend to contemplation. In such an institute there must be some place for works of the contemplative life. Hence "mixed" orders is not an inaccurate term after all. *Qui vult finem vult media ad finem. Nemo dat quod non habet.* [Whoever wants a goal also wants what is half-way toward that goal. No one gives what he does not have.]

7. "*In St. Thomas the degree of union with God has nothing to do with this problem.*" The concrete union of individual with God—*concedo.* But this institute must by its nature supply a reservoir upon which teachers and preachers are to draw. In other words, it must, by statute, favor union with God and works of the contemplative life.

8. I do not attempt to prove the Cistercians are a mixed order!!!!

9. "*An ecstasy is not a work of the active life.*" *Concedo prorsus.* [I absolutely agree.]

January 26, 1949. Feast of St. Alberic

When all that has been said, I am very glad they wrote that article because it has been an immense help to me. Yesterday I read St. Thomas' explanation of what he means by a "state"—that it is not a matter of external and accidental things, like poverty or riches, dignity or the rest, but rather a permanent disposition of a man in accordance with some mode proper to his nature, here by virtue of an obligation—*quod pertinet ad rationem libertatis vel servitutis. Ad statum requiritur immobilitas in eo quod pertinet ad conditionem personae* [what pertains to the reason for freedom or servitude. For a "state" to exist there is required an immobility in what pertains to the condition of the person] (*Summa Th.* II-II, Q. 183, a.1.).

In Q. 184, a.4., he explains in what sense he is taking the word state here.

Not—with regard to man's interior dispositions (v.g., a *state of* prayer) *spiritualis status in homine per comparationem ad judicium divinum* [a spiritual state in man by comparison to the divine judgment]

But—his exterior condition in relation to the rest of the Church— *secundum ea quae exterius aguntur accipitur spiritualis status in homine per comparationem ad Ecclesiam* [according to those things which are done externally, a spiritual state is accepted in man by comparison to the Church].

And he concludes: *Sic nunc de statibus loquimur prout sc. ex diversitate statuum quaedam Ecclesiae pulchritudo consurgit.* [We are now speaking of states in this manner because from the diversity of states there emerges a certain beauty of the Church.]

To see by this, with finality and certitude, just what St. Thomas was talking about, and how I had been wrong, was a great relief and brought much light. And far from obstructing my ideas, it helps me to see my own way much more clearly. I see how I can arrive at a more correct theological argument for the primacy of contemplation even in the mixed life. Also, I cannot do better than base everything I write ultimately on St. Thomas. In the first place, I don't understand Scotus and, even if I did, he does not carry enough weight as an authority. I have never been able to use him for anything anyway, and it seems to me the time I spent walking around the cemetery with the big black Vivés edition [1891] of the *Oxoniense* under my arm was largely wasted, although he does say some marvelous things about love. St. Thomas, on the other hand, is so clear and he has the whole Church behind him. The things that do not appeal to me immediately here and there will probably show up in their true light if I study the questions in relation to one another and to the whole *Summa* instead of simply plucking out isolated texts, and pulling them to pieces like daisies, "he loves me, he loves me not."

Anyway, one of the big graces of yesterday was seeing in a flash how much there is in the plan of the *Summa*, how much more the parts mean in relation to that whole. Never having seen this before,

I had never before really known anything about St. Thomas or the *Summa*, except isolated pieces of information. I had resolved not to do anything about *The Thomist* article saying, *Mihi vindictam* [*ego retribuam*] *dicit Dominus* ["Revenge is mine, I will repay, saith the Lord" (Romans 12:9)], and maybe this is His revenge—to give me a little understanding and the conviction of how much lies hidden in St. Thomas for me. *Pulsate et aperietur vobis.* [Knock, and it shall be opened for you (Matthew 7:7).] It is as if the *Summa* were some kind of Sacrament, working *ex opere operato* [solely by its own power]! Incidentally the Thomist position on the mode of causality of the Sacraments seems to me (without any investigation of the other views) to be the only one acceptable. That is, it makes an immediate appeal.

Bibliography

Works by Thomas Merton

The Ascent to Truth. New York: Harcourt, Brace, 1951.

Cistercian Contemplatives: A Guide to Trappist Life. Trappist, KY: Abbey of Gethsemani, 1948.

The Climate of Monastic Prayer. Washington, DC: Cistercian Publications, 1969.

Contemplation in a World of Action. Garden City, NY: Doubleday, 1971.

The Courage for Truth: Letters to Writers. Edited by Christine M. Bochen. New York: Farrar, Straus & Giroux, 1993.

Entering the Silence: Becoming a Monk and Writer. Journals, vol. 2: *1941–1952*. Edited by Jonathan Montaldo. San Francisco: HarperCollins, 1996.

Exile Ends in Glory: The Life of a Trappistine, Mother M. Berchmans, O.C.S.O. Milwaukee, WI: Bruce, 1948.

Figures for an Apocalypse. New York: New Directions, 1947.

Guide to Cistercian Life. Trappist, KY: Abbey of Gethsemani, 1948.

The Inner Experience: Notes on Contemplation. Edited by William H. Shannon. San Francisco: HarperCollins, 2003.

An Introduction to Christian Mysticism: Initiation into the Monastic Tradition 3. Edited by Patrick F. O'Connell. Kalamazoo, MI: Cistercian Publications, 2008.

A Man in the Divided Sea. New York: New Directions, 1946.

New Seeds of Contemplation. New York: New Directions, 1961.

The Road to Joy: Letters to New and Old Friends. Edited by Robert E. Daggy. New York: Farrar, Straus & Giroux, 1989.

Seasons of Celebration. New York: Farrar, Straus & Giroux, 1965.

Seeds of Contemplation. New York: New Directions, 1949.

Selected Essays. Edited by Patrick F. O'Connell. Maryknoll, NY: Orbis, 2013.

The Seven Storey Mountain. New York: Harcourt, Brace, 1948.

The Spirit of Simplicity. Trappist, KY: Abbey of Gethsemani, 1948.

The Tears of the Blind Lions. New York: New Directions, 1949.

Thirty Poems. Norfolk, CT: New Directions, 1944.

Thomas Merton on St. Bernard. Kalamazoo, MI: Cistercian Publications, 1980.

The Waters of Siloe. New York: Harcourt, Brace, 1949.

What Is Contemplation? Holy Cross, IN: Saint Mary's College, 1948; rev. ed. Springfield, IL: Templegate, [1950], 1981.

Witness to Freedom: Letters in Times of Crisis. Edited by William H. Shannon. New York: Farrar, Straus & Giroux, 1994.

Works by Others

Chautard, Jean-Baptiste. *The Soul of the Apostolate*. Translated by Thomas Merton. Trappist, KY: Abbey of Gethsemani, 1946.

Eudes, St. John. *The Life and Kingdom of Jesus in Christian Souls*. Translated by Thomas Merton. New York: P. J. Kenedy & Sons, 1946.

Luce, Clare Boothe, ed. *Saints for Now*. New York: Sheed & Ward, 1952.

O'Brien, John A., ed. *Where I Found Christ*. Garden City, NY: Doubleday, 1950.